C000120872

THE TRUE POMPEY FAN'S
MISCELLANY

THE TRUE POMPEY FAN'S MISCELLANY

JOHN PFC WESTWOOD
WITH MATT WHITTLE & IAN WILLIAMS

WITH A FORWORD BY
ANDY AWFORD

First published in hardback in Great Britain 2007
By Pennant Books
A division of Pennant Publishing Ltd

British Library Cataloguing-in-Publication Data:
A catalogue record for this book is available from
The British Library

ISBN 978-0-9550394-8-5

Design & Typeset by Envy Design Ltd

Printed and bound in Great Britain by
Creative Print & Design, Ebbw Vale, Wales

Pennant Books Ltd
A division of Pennant Publishing Ltd
PO Box 5071
Hove, BN52 9BB

— ACKNOWLEDGMENTS —

The production of this book would not have been possible without the help and valuable assistance of many kinds and we the authors would like to express our gratitude and thanks to the following; Basher Benfield, Tony Crausaz and Helen Crausaz, Bob Whittle (Bob's poems), Keith Barnes (Artwork), Brian Belton (author of *West Ham United Miscellany*), Julia Rowley (photographer), Andy Burton (www.kitclassics.co.uk), Graeme Andrew of Envy Design, Mary Tobin (copy editor) plus a special mention to Lisa Whittle, thank you.

Special thanks also to the Pompey Supporters Central Branch and Paul Banks.

In addition, we would like to give our heartfelt thanks to Andy Awford for the wonderful book foreword

Finally, a particular word of thanks to the Fratton Faithful and the number of individuals who gave us information on the end of the phone and bags of encouragement.

If there are any names we have failed to credit either in the book text or Bibliography, we apologise and ask that they contact our publishers.

JC
REMO
POMPEY
Play up Pompey!

— FOREWORD – ANDY AWFORD —

I have known John Westwood since I arrived at Portsmouth as a fresh-faced 16-year-old boy, making my debut at home to Crystal Palace on 15 April 1989, and, whenever you think of Pompey, you do think of Johnny Westwood. A few years ago, watching the *Match of the Day* credits play out on the TV, all I seem to remember is this image of Johnny Westwood ringing his bell. He is very popular and is the heartbeat of the Fratton End. If there is a noise that needs making within the ground, then John is the man to make it; he gets everything going and, if the lads are 1–0 down or are 0–0 and struggling, John will whip the crowd up with his bell, aided by his mates with the drums of course, and they get it all going. As anyone knows, there is no better place for crowd atmosphere than to play at Fratton Park and Mr Johnny Westwood has played a major part in all that.

One game I remember was the Stockport game at home in the 97–98 season. We were that many points adrift, and the club desperately needed a result. We got a 1–0 win, and they made as much noise that night as they ever have with just 8,500 people in the stadium, while these days they play to full houses of 20,000 fans. Johnny was instrumental in that as well, drumming up that support; he realised the problems we were in and got the support going.

Fair play to him, he is a credit to it all. He comes across as a bit loud and does the odd silly prank which gets the better of him at times, but deep down he is a nice fellow who is also articulate and has just got Pompey in his heart. Any mistakes that he does make he's quick to rectify and apologise, which is nice, but everything he does is meant in the right way. You know he would never harm anybody and I've got a lot of time for him. He's somebody I have known ever since I went to Pompey, and we have always kept in touch. The fans have always treated me well and obviously he is a big part of that.

I am proud to be asked to write this Foreword to the book. It will certainly test your knowledge on this proud club with its history, its triumphs and its defeats, as it is written with a true football fan's passion and emotion, plus the groans too! Hopefully, it will go well because it's a thoroughly entertaining read, and I wish him and the authors all the best with it.

Regards Andy Awford

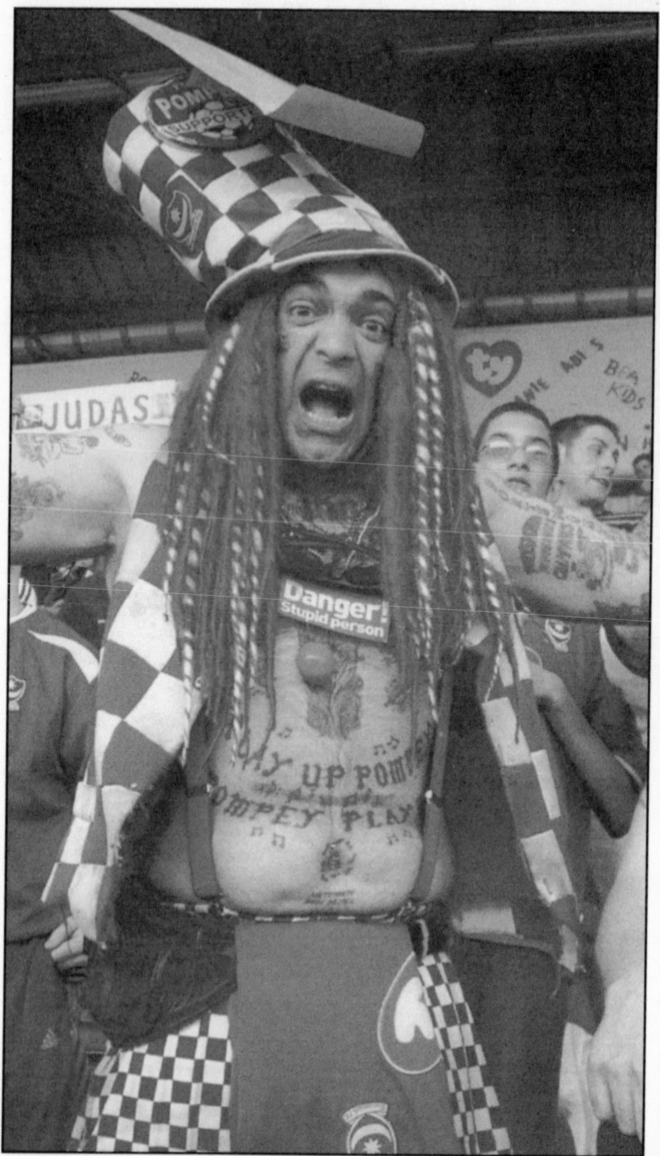
JUDAS
Danger!
Stupid person

— THE BASICS —

Address: Frogmore Road, Portsmouth PO4 8RA
Capacity: 20,288 (away supporters max. 3,000)
Stands: West Stand, North Stand, South Stand, Milton End (away supporters)
Programme: Chimes – Matchday Magazine

Contact Numbers:
Main Telephone: 02392 731204
Main Fax: 02392 734129
Ticket Office: 0871-230-1898
Ticket Office Fax: 0871-230-1899
Year Ground Opened: 1898
Pitch Size: 115 x 73 yards
Shirt Sponsors: OKI Printing Solutions
Home Kit Colours: Blue, White & Red
Away Kit Colours: White & Blue
Kit Manufacturers: JAKO
Official Website: www.pompeyfc.co.uk
Unofficial Websites: Pompey Till I Die
Pompey Online
Pompey-Fans.com

— GETTING THERE —

By Car:

From North and West:

Take M27 and M275 to the end, then take the 2nd exit at the roundabout and after ¼ mile turn right at the 'T' junction into London Road (A2047). After 1¼ miles, cross the railway bridge and turn left into Goldsmith Avenue. After ½ mile, turn left into Frogmore Road.

From East:

Take A27 following Southsea signs (A2030). Turn left at the roundabout (3 miles) on to A288, then right into Priory Crescent and next right into Carisbrooke Road.

By Rail:

Most trains to Pompey stop at Fratton BR Station. When you arrive, walk over the bridge and turn left into Goldsmith Avenue. Carry on till you reach Apsley Road and the visiting supporters' turnstiles are directly ahead.

By Bus (local):

13 – Commercial Road South, Fratton Bridge, Goldsmith Avenue, White House, Furze Lane.

17 – The Hard Interchange, Commercial Road, Victoria Road North/Elm Grove, Highland Road Post Office, White House, Goldsmith Avenue, Fratton Bridge, Commercial Road.

18 – Same route as 17.

Other services which stop close to the ground: 3, 13, 16, 16A, 24, 27 (all Fratton Bridge), 4, 4A, 6 (all Milton Road).

Pompey players born on 1 January

Robert (Bobby) Farrell b.1906; James (Jerry) Mackie b.1894; Brian Victor Snowdon b.1935; Alexander (Alec) Stenhouse b.1933

Pompey players born on 2 January

Robert Rodie (Bob) Dalrymple b.1880; John McColgan b.1900

— TRUE BLUE SONG —

To the tune of Tony Christie's 'Show Me the Way to Amarillo':

Shan-na-naa-naa-na-naa-na-na
Pommpee!
Shan-na-naa-naa-na-naa-na-na
Pommpee!
Shan-na-naa-naa-na-naa-na-na
*We went and sent S***hampton down.*

Pompey players born on 3 January

James Ferruer (Jimmy) Easson b.1906; Albert John Milkins b.1944; Thomas Rees b.1934

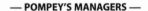

— POMPEY'S MANAGERS —

Pompey have hired a manager 29 times (about once every four-and-a-half years) but have had 27 managers:

1898 – Frank Brettell
1901 – Bob Blyth
1904 – Richard Bonney
1911 – Bob Brown
1920 – John McCartney
1927 – Jack Tinn
1947 – Bob Jackson
1952 – Eddie Lever
1958 – Freddie Cox
1961 – George Smith
1970 – Ron Tindall
1973 – John Mortimore
1974 – Ian St John
1977 – Jimmy Dickinson
1979 – Frank Burrows
1982 – Bobby Campbell
1984 – Alan Ball
1989 – John Gregory
1990 – Frank Burrows
1991 – Jim Smith
1995 – Terry Fenwick
1998 – Alan Ball
2000 – Tony Pulis
2000 – Steve Claridge
2001 – Graham Rix
2002 – Harry Redknapp
2004 – Velimir Zajec
2005 – Alain Perrin
2005 – Harry Redknapp

— MEMORABLE GAMES —

Chatham v Pompey (away!)
2 September 1899
Result: 0–1
Pompey goal scorer: Clarke

Approximately 4,000 witnessed Pompey, wearing salmon-pink shirts with maroon collars and cuffs, beat Chatham in their first League game in the Southern League Division One with a goal by Harold Clarke.

The News contained a brief match report and noted that most of the local supporters would have been satisfied with a draw, but when the news of their victory reached Pompey everyone was delighted.

Pompey's team sheet read as follows: M Reilly, H Turner, T Wilkie, R Blyth, H Stringfellow, T Cleghorn, R Marshall, D Cunliffe, A Brown, W Smith and H Clarke.

Pompey player born on 4 January
Leonard (Len) Beaumont b.1915

— TO THE FRATTON FAITHFUL —

The head may say 'don't go again, you know what's going to happen', but those with a team in their heart can't stay away. Play Up Pompey!

Die-hard fan Graeme Moir

Pompey player born on 5 January
Paul Anthony Gilchrist b.1951

Pomp & Posterity – 5 April 1898

Six men purchased five acres of land and founded Portsmouth FC.

Pompey players born on 6 January
Philip (Phil) Edward Gunter b.1932;
Leonard Thomas John Nash b.1911;
Reginald (Reg) Pickett b.1927

— TRUE BLUE SONG —

PLAY UP POMPEY
POMPEY PLAY UP!

Pompey player born on 7 January
Hugh Rainey b.1935

— TRUE BLUE FACTS —

Pompey's first kit was salmon-pink shirts with maroon cuffs and collars and white shorts, which earned them the nickname 'The Shrimps'. Now they'd look a bit like the 'Gay Pride XI'.

Portsmouth Football Club was created in 1898 when a group of local businessmen and sportsmen got together. Led by John 'The Brick' Brickwood (a local company owner), it was recorded with a Portsmouth-based solicitor that a piece of land close to Goldsmith Avenue, Portsmouth, would be purchased and used for the 'proposed football club'.

These men became the first directors of 'Portsmouth Football and Athletic Company Ltd' with 'Bricky' (Brickwood) as the club's first chairman.

Pompey player born on 8 January
Norman John Piper b.1948

Pompey players born on 9 January
Isaac (Ike) Clarke b.1915;
Bryan Lovell Dalton b.1917

— TRUE BLUE SONGS —

You are my Portsmouth, my only Portsmouth
You make me happy... when skies are grey,
You'll never notice... how much I love you,
Until you take... my Portsmouth... away
La, La, La, La, La... OHH.

I'm Portsmouth till I die
I'm Portsmouth till I die
I know I am, I'm sure I am
I'm Portsmouth till I die.

Pompey players born on 10 January
Redvern Esmond Edmunds b.1943;
Martin Kuhl b.1965;
Grahame Lloyd b.1951;
Joseph William (Bill) Spence b.1926

— TRUE BLUE FACTS —

Fratton Park was bought for the sum of £4,950.

For three successive seasons from 1977 to 1980, Pompey were drawn against Swindon Town in the League Cup and lost all three ties.

Three Pompey players – Mike Trebilcock in October 1970, Mark Hateley in November 1983 and Guy Whittingham in January 1991 – have scored double hat-tricks in the same month.

Pompey player born on 11 January
James (Jimmy) Scoular b.1925

— DO YOU KNOW WHERE WE'RE COMING FROM? —

Portsmouth Football Club was created largely from the local Royal Artillery team which had been suspended and subsequently disbanded. During their time, the RA club had gained promotion to the Southern Premier League and this success had caught the interest of local people who were now keen to watch first-class football in the city, in particular as S***hampton were now a successful, professional team. The first team manager to be appointed was Frank Brettell. With his experience of developing clubs such as Liverpool, Everton, Tottenham Hotspur and Bolton Wanderers, Brettell went about recruiting players, some of whom came from the disbanded RA club. The club then gained immediate entry to the Southern League.

Pompey players born on 12 January
Noel Lloyd George Blake b.1962;
Ivica Mornar b.1974;
Robert Prosinecki b.1969

Pomp & Posterity – 9 December 1899
The term 'Pompey' was first used in relation to Portsmouth FC.

Pompey player born on 13 January
James McWhirr b.1905

— TRUE BLUE FACTS —

In Pompey's first season, 1899/1900, they won 33 out of 53 competitive matches.

1998 was Pompey's Centenary Year.

A London War Cup was played during the Second World War. Pompey lost 2–0 in the final against Brentford in front of a Wembley gate of 72,000 fans.

Pompey players born on 14 January
Colin William Keir b.1938;
Marc Keller b.1968

— ORIGINS OF 'POMPEY' —

The epithet 'Pompey' has its origins in the Royal Navy, so it is naval, but its actual meaning is a matter of some dispute. Some claim it is derived from the 80-gun French warship *Le Pompee*, which was captured in 1793. She later fought with distinction in the battle of Algeciras in 1801 and was a guardship of Portsmouth Harbour.

But it is also argued that 'Pompey' was the product of a sailor's mind befuddled by drink. It was said that, during a talk by Agnes Weston, the naval temperance worker, the matlo woke from an alcoholic sleep amid a treatise on the Roman Empire and heard of the exploits of the general Pompey. On learning of the great man's death, the still inebriated Jack Tar cried out, 'Poor old Pompey!'

Another, perhaps more authentically naval, root of 'Pompey' places the word's origins in 1781. At this time, a group of British sailors with links to the naval dockyards in Portsmouth scaled Pompey's Pillar near Alexandria. From the top of the 98ft-high monument, they raised a bottle of punch to salute their climb. Their feat soon became common knowledge throughout the Royal Navy and beyond, and as their tale was told and retold they were referred to as 'The Pompey Boys'.

However, the most mundane yet the most likely reason why Portsmouth FC carries the epithet 'Pompey' (as a nationally recognised nickname) is the team's association with one Isaac George Martin, who was a professional with the club between 1911 and 1920, with a break during the First World War. Having been born in Gateshead, he came to Fratton Park from Sunderland and moved to Norwich in 1920. He was something of a naval hero (or at least that is how he was portrayed) and was known everywhere he went by the moniker 'Pompey', which denoted his alleged distinguished service. Isaac was something of a 'PR' figure for the club and was pushed forward to represent the nature and values of Portsmouth FC, although he never broke into the first team. In time, his nickname and the club became synonymous.

— SEASON 1899–1900 SOUTHERN LEAGUE DIVISION 1 —

Date		Team	Result	Gate
02 Sept	A	Chatham	W 1–0	4000
09 Sept	H	Reading	W 2–0	9000
16 Sept	A	Sheppey Utd	D 0–0	
23 Sept	H	Brighton Utd	W 3–1	6000
07 Oct	H	Bristol R	W 8–2	7000
28 Oct	H	Swindon	W 2–1	10000
04 Nov	A	New Brompton	L 0–1	
11 Nov	H	Gravesend	W 2–1	4693
25 Nov	H	Bristol C	W 2–0	6000
02 Dec	A	Cowes	W 4–0	
16 Dec	A	Millwall	L 1–2	
23 Dec	H	QPR	W 5–1	
25 Dec	A	Tottenham	L 0–3	15000
26 Dec	H	Bedminster	W 2–0	11000
30 Dec	H	Chatham	W 2–0	3500
06 Jan	A	Reading	L 0–2	
13 Jan	H	Sheppey Utd	W 3–0	4000
20 Jan	A	Brighton Utd	W 2–1	
03 Feb	A	Bedminster	L 0–2	
10 Feb	A	Bristol R	L 0–4	
24 Feb	H	Thames Ironworks	W 2–0	3500
03 Mar	H	Tottenham	W 1–0	4000
10 Mar	H	New Brompton	W 5–1	5000
17 Mar	A	Gravesend	W 1–0	
24 Mar	H	Swindon	W 1–0	4000
31 Mar	A	Bristol C	W 6–3	
05 Apr	A	Thames Ironworks	W 4–2	
14 Apr	A	S***hampton	W 2–0	4000
21 Apr	H	Millwall	W 2–0	6000
30 Apr	A	Swindon	L 1–3	
07 May	A	QPR	W 4–2	
16 May	H	S***hampton	W 2–0	1000

P28 W20 D1 L7 F58 A28 Pts 41
League Position: 2nd

Appearances: M Reilly 30; H Turner 6; T Wilkie 23; R Blyth 29; H Stringfellow 28; T Cleghorn 25; R G Marshall 30; D Cunliffe 28; A Brown 23; W Smith 27; H Clarke 28; E Turner 24; J Brown 6; G Barnes 8; J Hunter 9; R Struthers 9; F Moore 2; Harms 1

Pompey players born on 15 January

Michael Jean Elie Gaillard b.1927;
Kevin Patrick Harper b.1976;
Darryl Anthony Powell b.1971;
William Henry (Billy) Probert b.1893

Pomp & Posterity – 2 September 1899

Pompey's first League match took place and resulted in a 1–0 away win against Chatham. Three days later, Pompey made their home debut at Fratton Park against local rivals S***hampton. The visitors were defeated 2–0. In this first season, Pompey enjoyed huge success, winning 20 out of 28 League matches and finished runners-up in the Southern League.

Pompey players born on 16 January

Alexander (Alex) James Cropley b.1951;
Lee Alexander Molyneaux b.1983;
Trevor William Ross b.1957

Pomp & Posterity – Summer 1900

Fratton Park was completed at a cost of £6,538.

Pompey players born on 17 January

Vincent William (Billy) Clarke b.1911;
John (Jackie) Gillespie Henderson b.1932

Pompey player born on 18 January

Nicholas (Nicky) Jennings b.1946

Pompey players born on 19 January

Dennis Edwards b.1937;
Ronald (Rob) Vernon Newman b.1934;
James Mackrell b.1909

— THE TEAM BEHIND THE TEAM —

Owner: Alexandre Gaydamak
Directors: Mark Johnson, Peter Storrie, Roberto Avondo, Alexandre Gaydamak
Chief Executive: Peter Storrie
Manager: Harry Redknapp
Assistant Manager: Tony Adams
First Team Coach: Joe Jordan
Technical Director: Avraham Grant
Goalkeeping Coach: David Coles
Reserve Team Coach: Paul Groves
Head of Youth Development: Mark Kelly
Youth Team Coach: Shaun Brookes
Youth Development and Recruitment: Dave Hurst, Steve Martin
Chief Scout: Ian Broomfield

Pomp & Posterity – 1901–02

Pompey won the League for the first time in the 1901/02 season. By this time, Frank Brettell had been replaced as manager by former captain Bob Blyth (who was appointed on 7 January 1901).

Other highlights of this era included a famous 2–1 win over Manchester United in the FA Cup replay (1906/07 season), three seasons unbeaten at home and a first four-figure attendance that raised gate money of £24,329 (versus Manchester United).

Pompey players born on 20 January

Frederick C (Freddie) Cook b.1902;
David (Dave) Alfred Dodson b.1940;
Derek Alexander Dougan b.1938;
Allan Kane b.1957

Pompey player born on 21 January

John Lindsay Collins b.1949

Pomp & Posterity – 18 October 1902

Pompey's first home defeat was against Northampton, 0–1.

Pompey players born on 22 January
Leslie Charles (Charlie) Albert Dore b.1931;
Jonathon (Jon) Antoni Gittens b.1964;
Alexander (Alex) Kane b.1900

Pompey player born on 23 January
William George Lewry b.1896

— TRUE BLUE FACTS —

In May 1907, Pompey went on a tour of Germany and Austria.

Striker Billy Haines scored a hat-trick when beating Notts County 9–1 in 1927 to record Pompey's best-ever League win.

One goal cost Pompey promotion to the newly formed Premiership League in 1992 when goal difference gave West Ham United the runner-up spot with both clubs on 88 points.

Pompey player born on 24 January
John William Anderson b.1878

POMPEY PUB
The Newcombe Arms
Newcombe Road, Fratton

Pompey players born on 25 January
Michael Robert Brown b.1977; Jason Andre Davis Roberts b.1978;
Eustathis (Stathis) Tavlaridis b.1980

Pomp & Posterity – 21 January 1903
C B Fry, top-class cricketer, rugby player, athlete, international politician and forebear of comedian, actor and raconteur Stephen Fry, played his first match for Pompey.

Pompey players born on 26 January
Brian Lewis b.1943;
James Couttie Nichol b.1908

— TO THE FRATTON FAITHFUL —

I love it at Fratton Park. I love how intimidating it is and I love the 'Pompey Chimes' when they ring out.

Neil Warnock, 2003

— THE POMPEY CHIMES —

Although used by numerous other clubs over the years, the best-known chant sung out by the supporters of Portsmouth FC is the 'Pompey Chimes' ('Play up Pompey, Pompey play up' sung to the tune of the 'Westminster Chimes'). The most popular idea about the origins of this chorus is that it was 'transferred' from the Royal Artillery, the City of Portsmouth's most popular and successful football team for much of the 1890s. They played many of their home games at the United Services ground in Burnaby Road. The nearby Guildhall clock would strike the quarter hours and the referees would use the clock to let them know when the match should finish, at that time at 4pm. Just before this point was reached, the crowd would sing along with the chimes of the hour, perhaps hoping to influence the referee to blow the whistle signifying full-time (were the RA that bad?). One of the first recorded instances of Portsmouth fans' use of the Chimes are the words printed in the *1900/01 Official Handbook of Portsmouth FC*. They read: 'Play up Pompey, Just one more goal! Make tracks! What ho! Hallo! Hallo!'

It is said that, when the Royal Artillery were expelled from the 1898/99 FA Amateur Cup for alleged professionalism, many of the Royal Artillery's supporters moved their allegiance to the newly formed Portsmouth FC and brought the Chimes with them.

However, if you listen to the chimes in Guildhall Square, you will notice the difference between that melody and the tune traditionally adhered to by Portsmouth fans. It is argued by some that this is because the Chimes were first used by the supporters of a football team called St Mary's Church Young Men's Association, founded 15 years before the words of the Chimes appeared in the *Pompey Handbook*, and that the Chimes, in their original incarnation, were in tune with the bells of St Mary's. St Mary's was the club that would become S***hampton FC. According to Charlie Charles from East London, whose father was present at several of St Mary's home matches, the song had two variations starting 'Play up Mary's' and 'Play up the Saints'.

Pompey player born on 27 January
Frank Beddingfield b.1877

Pomp & Posterity – Summer 1904
Bob Blyth replaced by Richard Bonney as manager.

Pompey players born on 28 January
Derek Showers b.1953;
Kenneth (Kenny) Swain b.1952

Pompey player born on 29 January
James (Jim) Bell b.1885

Pomp & Posterity – 4 February 1905
Pompey won 2–0 in the FA Cup v First Division Small Heath (Manchester United to be).

Pompey players born on 30 January
Peter James Crouch b.1981;
Robert (Bobby) William Thomas Stokes b.1951

— POMPEY 100 CLUB —

(100+ League goals scored)

Peter Harris – 193 goals
John Weddle – 170 goals
Ron Saunders – 140 goals
Duggie Reid – 129 goals
Billy Haines – 119 goals
Ray Hiron – 110 goals
Johnny Gordon – 105 goals
Jimmy Easson – 102 goals

Pompey player born on 31 January
Robert Bishop b.1900

Pomp & Posterity – 28 April 1906
Pompey finished third in Division One of the Southern League.

Pompey players born on 1 February
John David (Dave) Bamber b.1959;
John A (Jack) Harwood b.1890

— STAR & CRESCENT HERO – CHRIS BURNS —

Brickie Burns became something of a cult hero at Fratton Park after his amazing rise from non-League football into Pompey's first team.

Chris was a bricklayer playing for Cheltenham Town at the start of 1991. By April 1992, he had played a full season in Pompey's first team and was playing in an FA Cup semi-final against Liverpool at Highbury.

Pompey first noticed Chris when he scored five goals for Cheltenham against Alvechurch in a Midland Floodlit Cup game. Then manager Frank Burrows was approached by one of Chris's teammates who suggested he take Chris on trial. Burrows agreed and, in March 1991, 'Burnsie' signed for Pompey at the age of 23 for a fee of around £25,000.

The 1991–92 season began with Jim Smith in charge and Chris was thrown straight into the first team along with other rising young stars such as Andy Awford, Kit Symons and Darren Anderton. While Burnsie may not have possessed the same skill as, say, Darren Anderton, his sweet left foot and work rate made him a favourite amongst fans.

In all, Chris ran out in 57 out of 58 competitive games that season on the left of midfield, scoring nine goals, and played an integral role in the FA Cup run.

However, the 1992–93 season saw Chris lose his place in the first team, and his career never fully recovered. He moved on to Northampton Town in April 1995, and in October 1996 he finally left the professional game and returned to the West Country to play for Gloucester City, where, after a spell at Forest Green Rovers, he returned to become player-manger in June 2001.

Pompey player born on 2 February
William (Bill) Kennedy b.1912

Pomp & Posterity – 12 January 1907
24,329 watched Pompey draw 2–2 with Man Utd in the FA Cup.

Pompey player born on 3 February
John Latimer b.1905

— AND SO THEY SAID ABOUT ME... —

In the KJC Stand was Pompey's most famous fan, John PFC Westwood, and his mates, banging their drums, blowing their bugles and leading the dedicated choir of followers in a hymn of praise to the team in blue.

The *Observer*

Thank God he didn't change his surname. I couldn't handle the name Mrs Football Club.

Mrs Westwood after the news he had legally changed his name to John Anthony Portsmouth Football Club Westwood

He has agreed that if we have any children they won't be called Fratton End or North Terrace.

A worrying afterthought from Mrs Westwood

Most were helpful but they were let down by the ones who threw out Westwood and friends for making too much noise. I ask you!

Travelling Pompey fan's view on Manchester City stewards

Oscar (a Pompey-supporting toy monkey) who accompanies him everywhere was kidnapped. The monkey was targeted by a splinter group of fans that idolise Blues coach Dave Kemp, after Westwood failed to stir the Fratton End into a chant of 'Dave Kemp's Blue and White Army'. He has until the next game to raise the chant or the toy monkey gets beheaded at 5pm.

***The News*: 'Troubled times for Westwood'**

Blackburn away

The excitement of one uneventful season saw Westwood's rattle confiscated at Blackburn accompanied by chants of 'The Old Bill's nicked me rattle'. After singing the song for the lamented rattle for about 10 minutes, the remaining Pompey faithful were so moved by John's traumatic experience they burst into 'The old bill nicked his rattle, la, la, la, la...'.

Brighton away

Another Pompey defeat, soaked to the skin and Seaweed taunting as they left their covered enclosure. Suddenly, from over the other side of the ground, a distant clicking was heard. The noise grew louder and Westwood was revealed, swaggering nonchalantly with not a care in the world towards ranks of Pompey fans who gave him the loudest chant of the night... 'There's only one Johnny Westwood!!!'

— TO THE FRATTON FAITHFUL —

A sure-fire sign that the world is coming to an end at Fratton Park is the sight of KJC Stand bugler John Westwood cradling a pint of water. The last time Westwood drank water was when he mistook it for a glass of vodka and tonic.

The News

— JOHN WESTWOOD'S DREAM TEAM XI —

Alan Knight

Glen Johnson Sol Campbell Linvoy Primus Matthew Taylor

Steve Stone Robert Prosinecki Pedro Mendes Patrik Berger

Ayegbeni Yakubu Guy Whittingham

Subs: David James, Gary O'Neil, Mark Hateley

Pompey player born on 4 February

John F Scott b.1909

Pomp & Posterity – 1908–09

Pompey's last season playing League games in pink and salmon colours.

Pompey players born on 5 February
John Aloisi b.1976; Daniel (Dan) Ekner b.1927;
Michael (Mike) Hazard b.1960;
Henriques Manuel Fernandes b.1986;
Eric Norman Jones b.1915

— STAR & CRESCENT HERO – ALAN BALL —

Pompey returned to the top flight for the first time in 28 years under the management of Alan Ball. Ballie joined Pompey in May 1984, and the following two seasons saw promotion near-misses with the team finishing fourth in the League on both occasions. Then, in the 1986/87 season, Ball took Pompey back into the Promised Land for the first time since the 1958/59 season.

When Alan Ball came to Pompey, he was already a household name, having had a distinguished playing career. He was the youngest member of the 1966 World Cup-winning England team, and he had significant spells with both Everton and Arsenal in the top League. Despite this success, his career got off to a shaky start after being rejected by Wolves, and then Bolton, for being 'too small'. Eventually, he was signed up by Blackpool as a favour to his dad. Ball was still playing for Blackpool when he got his first call-up to the England squad.

Ball was a popular manager at Pompey, and fans remember him as the manager that got the team promoted. Despite having subsequently managed S***hampton after being sacked by Pompey, Ball still got a warm welcome when he came on as a substitute in Alan Knight's testimonial game against S***hampton in 1996.

In February 1998, Ball came back to Pompey and inspired the team to another great escape, avoiding relegation to Division Two when it had seemed a foregone conclusion. Few who were there will forget *that* Stockport game when the chant of 'Alan Ball's Blue and White Army' rang out incessantly throughout the second half, spurring the team on to a 1–0 victory.

Ball certainly instilled a fighting spirit in the team with his management style, something that always appeals to the Fratton crowd, and he remains popular in Pompey, which is perhaps unique considering his associations with the team down the road!

Pompey player born on 6 February
Timothy (Tim) Alan Sherwood b.1969

— TRUE BLUE JOKE —

It is just before Pompey v S***hampton in an important south-coast derby. Pompey need the points to keep their place in Europe on track and S***hampton need the points to help them win their relegation battle. Ayegbeni Yakubu goes into the Pompey changing room to find all his teammates looking a bit glum. 'What's up?' he asks.

'Well, we're having trouble getting motivated for this game,' says Matty Taylor. 'We know it's important but it's only S***hampton. They're rubbish and we can't be bothered!'

The Yak looks at them and says, 'Well, I reckon I can beat these by myself, you lads go down the pub.'

So the Yak goes out to play S***hampton by himself and the rest of the Pompey team go off down the pub for a few beers.

After a few pints, the Pompey players wonder how the game is going, so they get the landlord to put the teletext on. Everyone in the pub lets out a big cheer as the screen reads:

Pompey 1 S***hampton 0
Yakubu 8 mins

He is beating S***hampton all by himself!

Anyway, a few pints later and the game is forgotten until Linvoy Primus suddenly remembers that the game must've finished by now. 'It must be full-time now. Let's see how he got on!'

They put the teletext on.

Result: Pompey 1 S***hampton 1
Yakubu 8 mins Beattie 90mins

Everyone lets out a big cheer!

The Pompey players can't believe it: the Yak has single-handedly got a draw against S***hampton!!!

They rush back to Fratton Park to congratulate him. They find him in the dressing room, still in his kit, sat with his head in his hands looking absolutely gutted!

'What's up?' asks Stevie Stone.

The Yak refuses to look at them. 'I've let you down. I've let you down.'

'Don't be daft, you got the draw against S***hampton, all by yourself and they only scored at the very end! You should be proud of yourself!'

'No, no, I have! I've let you down! I got sent off after 10 minutes!!!'

Pompey players born on 7 February

Peter John Walter Atyeo b.1932;
William (Billy) Shaun Murray b.1970;
Angus McLaren Meikie b.1900;
Solomon Upton b.1891

THE SOUTH-COAST DERBY HISTORY

	P	W	D	L
Southern League	32	12	5	15
Football League	26	6	8	12
Premiership League	4	2	0	2
FA Cup	4	0	0	4
League Cup	1	0	0	1
Total	**67**	**19**	**13**	**32**

Pompey player born on 8 February

Terence (Terry) Foley b.1938

Pompey player born on 9 February

Daniel (Dan) McPhail b.1903

Pompey players born on 10 February

Shirley Wray Abbott b.1889;
George Clifford b.1896

Pompey players born on 11 February

Neil John Ayrton b.1962;
Carl Tiler b.1970;
Arthur Mounteney b.1883

Pompey player born on 12 February

Thomas Henry (Tommy) Brown b.1896

DOUBLE AGENTS

*Players who have played for both S***hampton and Pompey*

John Bainbridge
Ian Baird
Dave Beasant
William Beaumont
John Beresford
Robert Blyth
Tommy Bowman
Arthur Brown
Arthur Chadwick
Mick Channon
Colin Clarke
Eammon Collins
Andy Cook
Peter Crouch
Ron Davies
Charles Burgess Fry
Paul Gilchrist
Mervyn Gill
Jon Gittens
Alex Glen
Ivan Golac
Willie Haines
Trevor Hebberd
Scott Hiley
Barry Horne
Ted Hough
Kelly Houlker
Bill Kennedy
George Lawrence
John Lewis
Alex McDonald
John McIlwaine
Jerry Mackie
Alan McLoughlin
Steve Middleton
George Molyneux
Harry Penk
Nigel Quashie
Matt Reilly
Matthew Robinson
Bill Rochford
Bobby Stokes
Issac Tomlinson
Malcolm Waldron
John Warner
Ernest Williams
Arthur Wood

Pompey players born on 13 February

David (Dave) Harry Pullar b.1959;
Steven (Steve) Charles Perrin b.1952

— ORIGINS OF THE TERM SCUMMER —

SCUM (SCUMMERS): A worthless person or contemptible person or group of people.

As with the term Pompey and the 'Pompey Chimes', the insult 'Scummer' has contested origin.

Some say it goes back to shortly before the First World War when there was a wage dispute between a local fishing company and its employees. The company had two sites, one in S***hampton and the other in Pompey. The union called a strike that was held by the Pompey men, but after a number of weeks the S***hampton fishingmen went back to work and the action collapsed with the employers not giving an inch. The men working out of Pompey were disgusted with their colleagues down the coast. It was at this point that it was noticed that the initials of the S***hampton Company Union Men was SCUM. Hence, the name Scum or Scummer as a term of abuse for anyone from S***hampton gained currency.

Another version of this legend proposes that 'Scummer' emanated from industrial action taken at Pompey and S***hampton docks. At the start of a strike, the Pompey dockers agreed with their comrades in S***hampton to close both ports to improve conditions and pay for the workers. However the S***hampton port secretly opened while Pompey was striking, and so took all the trade. The word 'Scum' was used to refer to S***hampton dockers and by association anyone who came from S***hampton (as everyone in the town benefited from the treachery), because it was an acronym of the S***hampton Community Union Members'. Pompey workers then referred to them as 'Scum', as being comparable to waste refuse, which evolved to 'Scummer'.

Pompey players born on 15 February

Ambrose Robert Brown b.1911;
Ernest (Ernie) James Howe b.1953;
Richard (Dick) John Reynolds b.1948

Pompey players born on 16 February

Samuel (Sammy) Edward Campbell Chapman b.1938;
David Ian Crown b.1958;
Malcolm Shotton b.1957

— TRUE BLUE JOKE —

S***hampton's manager was getting worried that all his players were rubbish, so he phoned Harry Redknapp for some advice. 'H' explained that he got all the Pompey players to dribble round cones, thus improving their close ball control. He suggested to their manager to try this.

Two weeks later, Redders rang back to see how the Saints manager and his coaches were coping with his tip. But their manager was still annoyed.

'Didn't my suggestion work?' asked a bemused Harry Redknapp.

The Saints manager's reply was full of anger and hurt: 'F***ing cones beat us 3-0!'

— GAMES AGAINST S***HAMPTON —

The Dell in 1902 – S*hampton 1 Pompey 1**

The Pompey contingent, which numbered upwards of a thousand, being easily distinguishable by their salmon-pink and maroon rosettes.

The Football Mail

3 January 1988 – S*hampton 0 Pompey 2**

A great day for Portsmouth Football Club, for the city of Portsmouth – and a bit special for me.

A chirpy Alan Ball, Pompey's manager

21 March 2004 – Pompey 1 S*hampton 0**

*Pompey's day in heaven started when there was a hailstorm that would have sent Noah scurrying for his ark smashing down on the uncovered visiting fans shortly before kick-off. To protect themselves the S***hampton supporters turned their backs on the pitch.*

The News

24 April 2005 – Pompey 4 S*hampton 1**

*S***hampton fans driving to Pompey were greeted with banners on the M27 reading 'Welcome to Hell'.*

How would you think it has been for me? Do you think that it has been a wonderful day for me or something? It has not been a good day!

Unhappy Saints manager Harry Redknapp, when asked after that defeat if it had been a tough day for him personally

— TRUE BLUE JOKE —

A little boy tok his parents to court because he did not want to live with them any more.

The judge said to him, 'Why don't you want to live with your dad?

'Because he beats me,' said the little boy.

'Why don't you live with your mum then?' asked the judge.

'Because she also beats me.'

'Oh', said the judge. 'Well who would you like to live with then?'

The little boy replied, 'I would like to live with S***hampton FC, because they don't beat anyone!!'

Pompey players born on 17 February
Reginald (Reg) Victor Cutler b.1935;
John William Whalley b.1897

Pompey players born on 18 February
Harold William Crawshaw b.1912;
William Derek Rees b.1934

Pomp & Posterity – 1909–10
Pompey first adopted white shirts, black shorts and socks for competitive games.

— TRUE BLUE FACT —

S***hampton was granted city status in 1964, 770 years later than Portsmouth, which was made a city by virtue of its Royal Charter in 1194.

Pompey player born on 19 February
James (Jamie) Alexander Howell b.1977

— A POEM BY BOB —

PFC – The Love of My Life
Every Time

Every time I write a verse
It's written just for you
Every time I see the Park
A smile comes shining through
Every time you come to mind
I feel it in my heart
Somehow I knew I'd fall for you
Even from the start
Every time that I'm alone
And working through the night
Reflect upon the script at hand
And try to get it right
Every time my spirit's low
You brighten up my day
Every time a match arrives
Can't wait to see you play
Every time I start to dream
My thoughts return to you
Every time I sit and think
I find my feelings true
Every time our heroes score
And every time we win
Every time the chips are down
Our chances looking thin
Every time I take my seat
And action starts to flow
Every time, Yes now it's time
To say I love you so.

PLAY UP POMPEY

— TRUE BLUE FACTS —

Percy Whitney was the club's first financial secretary.

Pompey's John Kerr achieved the unwelcome record of becoming the first ever substitute in the League to be substituted.

When Peter Marinello arrived from Arsenal and signed for Pompey in July 1973, he was hailed as the 'new George Best', and just like Bestie he never got to play in any World Cup Finals. Alas, the similarity ended there.

Pomp & Posterity – 1910–11

Pompey's bubble of success burst in 1910 when the club ran into financial difficulties and were relegated to the Southern Second Division. Although promotion was achieved the following season under new manager Bob Brown, Pompey were beginning to know what life in professional football was all about.

— KEEP YOUR TICKET STUBS —

Recently on eBay, a ticket from Pompey's 1934 FA Cup Final match with Manchester City sold for £133.09, having been originally purchased for 10/6 (52½ pence) back in 1934. This means that a £100 FA Cup Final ticket purchased today might be expected to go for £25,530 in the year 2078!! Can't wait!

Meanwhile, a matchday programme, originally purchased for 2½ pence was auctioned for £238.33. Again, equating to today's terms, a £10 FA Cup Final programme might fetch as much as £95,330 in 72 years' time.

Pompey players born on 20 February

Albert Laurence Juliussen b.1920;
David Michael Kemp b.1953;
James Kennedy b.1897;
Peter Marinello b.1950;
William Norman McCourt Uprichard b.1928

Pomp & Posterity – 1911–12

Financial difficulties continued during this period and a solution was found when the original company was wound up. Portsmouth City FC was then formed in 1911 and secured the future of the club.

Pompey adopted royal-blue shirts and white shorts for competitive games.

Pompey player born on 21 February
Cyril Hutton Rutter b.1933

— STAR & CRESCENT HERO – MARTIN KUHL —

Martin Kuhl was signed by Alan Ball in 1988 from Watford for a fee of £125,000 after Pompey had been relegated from the old First Division.

Martin's early career had seen him play under Jim Smith at Birmingham City, making his first-team debut at the age of 18 in 1983. He then moved on to Sheffield United and Watford.

Surprisingly, Martin struggled in his first few games and was not instantly a hit with the fans. However, after settling down, he went on to become one of the club's most consistent performers, and, by the time Pompey featured in the FA Cup semi-finals in April 1992, he was team captain.

He became popular with Pompey fans for his tireless work rate and lethal shot. He was a tough tackling midfielder who also had an eye for a pass, although, uncharacteristically, he was one of the unfortunate players to miss in the penalty shoot-out against Liverpool at Villa Park in the semi-final replay.

Kuhl was sold to Derby County at the start of the 1992–93 season for £650,000, much to the disgust of the fans. After Pompey missed out on promotion to the Premier League that season, to West Ham on goal difference, some fans looked back on the sale of Martin Kuhl and wondered if things would have been different had he stayed.

Pompey players born on 22 February
Neil Shaka Hislop b.1969; Joseph F (Joe) Potts b.1891;
Edward (Ted) Smith b.1902

Pomp & Posterity – 25 April 1914

Billy James scored 21 goals for Pompey in his first season playing for the club.

— HOMEGROWN POMPEY XI —

The following 11 players were all born in Pompey:

Name	Born
William Albury	10-08-1933
Kevin Bartlett	12-10-1962
John Gordon	11-09-1931
Raymond Crawford	13-07-1936
John Davies	26-09-1933
Steve Middleton	28-03-1953
Ralph Hunt	14-08-1933
Stephen Foster	24-09-1957
John Beale	16-10-1930
Clive Green	06-12-1957
Peter Harris	19-12-1925

Pompey players born on 23 February

James Stephen (Steve) Griffiths b.1914;
John Alexander (Alex) Mackie b.1903

Pompey players born on 24 February

Lloyd Anthony McGrath b.1965;
Philip (Phil) Stanley Roberts b.1950

Pomp & Posterity – 1915–16

A whirlwind ripped the roof off of the South Stand at Fratton Park.

Pompey players born on 25 February

Jeffrey (Jeff) Lawrence Hemmerman b.1955;
John Thomas McLaughlin b.1952

Pompey players born on 26 February

Alan Paul Biley b.1957; Ceri Morgan Hughes b.1971;
Miguel Pedro Mendes b.1979;
Fitzroy Simpson b.1970

Pomp & Posterity – First World War

The First World War saw football suspended and Pompey didn't resume playing until the 1919/20 season when Pompey won the Southern League for the second time.

— STAR & CRESCENT HERO – NOEL BLAKE —

Noel Blake was brought to the club by Alan Ball from Birmingham City for a fee of £150,000 in the summer of 1984. He was ever present in the promotion near-miss seasons of 1984/85 and 1985/86 and then the promotion season of 1986/87.

Before joining Pompey, Noel had done a tour of West Midlands clubs, starting his career at Walsall before moving on to Aston Villa, where he could only play a bit part in their European Cup-winning side. A more successful stop at Birmingham City was to follow before he joined Pompey.

After initially not settling in too well, with allegations of racial abuse made, Noel became a firm favourite with the fans, going on to win player of the year awards in the 1985/86 and 1986/87 seasons. It wasn't all easy, though, and Noel had some legendary misunderstandings with goalkeeper Alan Knight, resulting in four own goals in his first season!

Due to injury, Noel only played about half the season in the First Division, and, ultimately, Pompey were relegated. Noel went on to play for Leeds United, Stoke City, Bradford City and Dundee, before settling down in Exeter.

Pompey player born on 27 February
Harold Clarke b.1875

— TRUE BLUE FACT —

Arthur Knight played cricket for Hampshire, won 30 amateur caps at football for England, represented Great Britain at the 1912 Stockholm Olympics and won a full England cap while with Pompey.

Pompey player born on 28 February
John Cairns b.1902

Pompey player born on 29 February
James J (Jimmy) Burnett b.1880

Pompey players born on 1 March
Thomas (Tommy) David Curtis b.1973;
Robert (Bobby) Sydney William Kellard b.1943

— BEST SUPPORTERS IN THE LAND —

I had a bit of a headache by the end. Our fans never stopped singing the whole game.

Steve Stone after Wolves at home, 2003

Any mention of Fratton Park wouldn't be complete without a nod to the Portsmouth fans. For me, they are some of the best and most vocal fans in the League. They've had it tough this season but they still sing their hearts out and that will play a big part in helping them escape the drop if they can.

Gordon Davies, ex-Fulham player, on Pompey, 2006

The Pompey fans are real football supporters, they are not just looking at the players who score the goals, they watch the team as a team. It is nice to get the appreciation, like when they are chanting your name or give you a little cheer.

Arjan De Zeeuw, 2004

Pompey fans are well known for their passion and it's been no different this season. The backing we get both home and away is amazing and quite unique, and it's no wonder that they have been recognised at the club as our '12th man' and, in fact, been given a squad number of their own.

Linvoy Primus

Our fans at Bramall Lane were a credit to themselves. The atmosphere you generate is so important to us and gives all the playing staff a great buzz every time. We feel we always have a chance with supporters like ours behind us.

Darren Moore on Pompey's fans at Sheffield Utd, season 2000

Everybody in football knows about Pompey supporters and their fanatical support for their club.

Shaka Hislop

There are plenty of people who say to me, 'They are a bit mad.'

Sports commentator and Pompey fan Ian Darke

Our supporters were vocal, they always are, but I know they are not violent people and I am glad that showed yesterday.

Milan Mandaric after 4–1 defeat of S*hampton**

It's important they win at home where they've got the 12th man – the crowd – behind them.

City Council Leader Phil Shaddock

Even when I missed the penalty, the fans were still right behind us, and roaring us on. For them to sing my name after I missed the penalty was big stuff. They've been big all season.

Paul Merson, 2003

Pompey fans sing loudest and longest in the Premiership; according to a special survey, passionate Pompey supporters spend an average 58 minutes singing per match registering an ear-splitting 97 decibels.

www.fanchants.com

I have a bond with the supporters and it's a feeling that's never changed. I still get recognised in the town. Perhaps it's because of 'The Barnet'.

Alan Biley

After half-an-hour of watching Ipswich outclass Pompey, the chant of 'You're not very good' was directed at the visitors by the home supporters. No irony here, just prejudice.

The Daily Telegraph

28 October 1980 – League Cup 4th round
Liverpool 4 Pompey 1

Thirteen thousand supporters arrived by road and rail to yell themselves hoarse and force the celebrated Kop Choristers to play second fiddle on their own stomping ground; as the Pompey faithful greeted their team's appearance with a blizzard of shredded paper, the Kop stood open-mouthed.

— TO THE FRATTON FAITHFUL —

Supporters' club fan of the year 2000 was Barry Harris, the Pompey sailor for 20 years.

Pompey players born on 2 March
Warren David Hunt b.1984;
Giannis Ioannis Skopelitis b.1978

Pompey players born on 3 March
Darren Robert Anderton b.1972;
Robert (Robbie) Anthony Simpson b.1976;
George Harold Marshall b.1896

— TRUE BLUE FACTS —

In 1918, the US army beat the Canadians 4–3 in a game of baseball at Fratton Park.

Pompey and Huddersfield have a unique record in that both clubs have played each other in all four divisions bar the Premiership.

Pompey players born on 4 March
Wilfred (Wilf) McCoy b.1921;
John Edgar Phillips b.1937;
Garry Ernest Stanley b.1954;
Thomas James (Tom) Wren b.1907

POMPEY PUB
The Shepherd's Crook
Goldsmith Avenue, Southsea

Pompey players born on 5 March
James (Jimmy) Elder b.1928; John Bonar McCelland b.1935

— TRUE BLUE FACT —

Pompey's first league match in Division Three was at Fratton Park against Swansea on 28 August 1920 resulting in a 3-0 home victory

Pompey players born on 6 March
Robert (Bob) Kearney b.1903;
John Joseph Kerr b.1955

Pompey players born on 7 March
Andrew (Andy) Griffin b.1979; Ian Purdie b.1953

Pompey players born on 8 March
James Leslie (Jimmy) Bartram b.1911;
Ronald Barrington (Barry) Mansell b.1932;
Christopher (Kit) Jeremiah Symons b.1971

— SEASON 1920–21 LEAGUE DIVISION 3 —

Date		Team	Result	Gate
28 Aug	H	Swansea	W 3–0	20232
30 Aug	A	Luton	D 2–2	
04 Sept	A	Swansea	D 0–0	14000
08 Sept	H	Luton	W 3–0	14000
11 Sept	A	S***hampton	L 0–2	18000
15 Sept	H	Gillingham	D 1–1	8000
18 Sept	H	S***hampton	L 0–1	20585
25 Sept	H	Millwall	D 0–0	16000
02 Oct	A	Millwall	L 0–1	
09 Oct	A	Northampton	L 0–1	
16 Oct	H	Northampton	W 2–0	15000
23 Oct	A	Newport Co	L 0–1	
30 Oct	H	Newport Co	L 0–2	13679
06 Nov	A	Southend	L 1–2	
13 Nov	H	Southend	W 3–0	13729
27 Nov	H	Gillingham	D 2–2	14718
11 Dec	H	Merthyr Town	D 0–0	12719
18 Dec	H	Swindon Town	D 1–1	11111
25 Dec	A	Watford	L 2–3	
27 Dec	H	Watford	W 1–0	25173
01 Jan	A	Swindon Town	L 2–5	
15 Jan	H	Reading	D 2–2	14160
22 Jan	A	Reading	L 0–1	
05 Feb	H	Plymouth	D 1–1	12357
12 Feb	H	Bristol Rov	W 1–0	13966
19 Feb	A	Bristol Rov	D 2–2	12000
21 Feb	A	Merthyr Town	L 1–2	12000

26 Feb	H	Brentford	L	0–2	13645
05 Mar	A	Brentford	W	2–1	
12 Mar	H	Norwich	W	2–1	12128
19 Mar	A	Norwich	D	2–2	
25 Mar	H	Exeter City	W	2–1	19701
26 Mar	A	C Palace	L	0–3	18000
28 Mar	A	Exeter City	D	0–0	10000
09 Apr	A	Brighton	L	0–3	
13 Apr	A	Plymouth	L	0–2	11000
16 Apr	H	Brighton	W	3–0	13599
23 Apr	A	Grimsby	W	3–0	10000
30 Apr	H	Grimsby	W	2–1	13697
02 May	A	QPR	D	0–0	
07 May	H	QPR	D	0–0	14933

P42 W12 D15 L15 F46 A48 Pts 39
League Position 12th

Appearances: E R Robson 41; W Probert 42; A E Knight 28; H Buddery 17; J Harwood 29; J Turner 22; E Thompson 36; F Stringfellow 37; J Armstrong 13; W James 22; B A Youtman 1; T Newton 1; H J Frampton 3; J Cumming 8; S Abbott 23; J A Hogg 15; J Mackie 6; J Reid 7; W Beedie 21; J Potts 5; D Coid 7; J B Brown 24; J Martin 16; J W Smelt 1; D Watson 13; W G Lewry 4; P Cherrett 7; H J Leavey 13

— TRUE BLUE SONG —

And it's Portsmouth City,
Portsmouth City FC
We're by far the greatest city
The world has ever seen.

— TRUE BLUE FACT —

The area called Fratton in Pompey was originally known as Froddington.

Pomp & Posterity – 1920/21

The club continued to succeed when they joined the newly formed National Football League Third Division. The debut season in this League saw the club finish in 12th position.

Pompey player born on 9 March
Thomas (Tom) Clehorn b.1871

1920–21 League Division Three (South)												
	P	W	D	L	F	A	W	D	L	F	A	Pts
1 Crystal Palace	42	15	4	2	45	17	9	7	5	25	17	59
2 S***hampton	42	14	5	2	46	10	5	11	5	18	18	54
3 QPR	42	14	4	3	38	11	8	5	8	23	21	53
4 Swindon Town	42	14	5	2	51	17	7	5	9	22	32	52
5 Swansea City	42	9	10	2	32	19	9	5	7	24	26	51
6 Watford	42	14	4	3	40	15	6	4	11	19	29	48
7 Millwall	42	11	5	5	25	8	7	6	8	17	22	47
8 Merthyr Town	42	13	5	3	46	20	2	10	9	14	29	45
9 Luton Town	42	14	6	1	51	15	2	6	13	10	41	44
10 Bristol Rovers	42	15	3	3	51	22	3	4	14	17	35	43
11 Plymouth Argyle	42	10	7	4	25	13	1	14	6	10	21	43
12 Pompey	**42**	**10**	**8**	**3**	**28**	**14**	**2**	**7**	**12**	**18**	**34**	**39**
13 Grimsby Town	42	12	5	4	32	16	3	4	14	17	43	39
14 Northampton Town	42	11	4	6	32	23	4	4	13	27	52	38
15 Newport County	42	8	5	8	20	23	6	4	11	23	41	37
16 Norwich City	42	9	10	2	31	14	1	6	14	13	39	36
17 Southend Utd	42	13	2	6	32	20	1	6	14	12	41	36
18 Brighton HA	42	11	6	4	28	20	3	2	16	14	41	36
19 Exeter City	42	9	7	5	27	15	1	8	12	12	39	35
20 Reading	42	8	4	9	26	22	4	3	14	16	37	31
21 Brentford	42	7	9	5	27	23	2	3	16	15	44	30
22 Gillingham	42	6	9	6	19	24	2	3	16	15	50	28

Pompey players born on 10 March

Matthew (Matt) Gemmell b.1931;
Pavel Srnicek b.1968

Pomp & Posterity – 1921–22

Pompey finished third in League Division Three.

Pompey players born on 11 March

Thomas Casey b.1930;
Paul George Hardyman b.1944;
Charles Joseph (Joe) Quinn b.1902

— BLUES —

Players that have played for both Pompey and Birmingham

John Beresford
Noel Blake
Lee Bradbury
Steve Bryant
Mark Burchill
Steve Claridge
Liam Daish
Kevin Dearden
Kevin Dillon
John Gordon
Andy Gosney
Alex Govan
Ian Hendon
Scott Hiley
Barry Horne
Roger Jones
Martin Kuhl
Arthur Mounteney
Darryl Powell
Herbert Powell
John Shufflebotham
George Smith
Arthur Styles
Carl Tiler
George Wheldon

Pompey player born on 12 March
Amdy Mustapha Faye b.1977

— TRUE BLUE FACT —

Pompey oldest recorded player is George Wheldon who was born in 1869.

Pompey players born on 13 March
John McCrae Kirk b.1930;
Martin John Phillips b.1976

Pomp & Posterity – 1922–23
William 'Farmer's Boy' Haines joined Pompey.

Pompey player born on 14 March
Walter S Cookson b.1881

— STAR & CRESCENT HERO – WILLIAM 'BILLY' HAINES —

Haines joined Pompey after manager John McCartney was contacted by a fan who had seen him play at Frome Town while on holiday.

He was brought to Pompey and played for the reserves where he scored consistently, prompting his first-team debut at home to Swindon Town on 30 March 1923 where he scored in a 4–1 victory.

Haines went on to score regularly for the team and became the record holder of the most goals scored in a season (40 in the 1926/27 season) until a certain Guy Whittingham came along (42 goals in the 1992/1993).

Billy was a fans' favourite and scored an impressive 119 goals in 164 League appearances.

Pompey players born on 15 March
Henry (Harry) Abbot b.1895;
Gianluca Festa b.1969

— TRUE BLUE FACTS —

Pompey full-back Arthur Knight's middle name was Egerton.

Pompey, along with Luton and Notts County, are one of the only three clubs who have been relegated from the First to the Fourth Division, then gained promotion all the way back to the First Division.

In the 1980–81 season, at home to Exeter Mick Tait scored the fastest ever hat-trick in Pompey history – 62, 64, 65 minutes.

Pompey player born on 16 March
C Frederick William Fred Cook b.1880

Pomp & Posterity – 1923–24

Pompey won the League in 1923/24 season greatly assisted by Billy Haines scoring 28 League goals in 31 matches. By this time manager Bob Brown had been replaced by John McCartney from Hearts.

Pompey player born on 17 March
William (Willie) Cooper b.1890

1923–24 League Division Three (South)													
		P	**W**	**D**	**L**	**F**	**A**	**W**	**D**	**L**	**F**	**A**	**Pts**
1	**Pompey**	**42**	**15**	**3**	**3**	**57**	**11**	**9**	**8**	**4**	**30**	**19**	**59**
2	Plymouth Argyle	42	13	6	2	46	15	10	3	8	24	19	55
3	Millwall	42	17	3	1	45	11	5	7	9	19	27	54
4	Swansea City	42	18	2	1	39	10	4	6	11	21	38	52
5	Brighton HA	42	16	4	1	56	12	5	5	11	12	25	51
6	Swindon Town	42	14	5	2	38	11	3	8	10	20	33	47
7	Luton Town	42	11	7	3	35	19	5	7	9	15	25	46
8	Northampton Town	42	14	3	4	40	15	3	8	10	24	32	45
9	Bristol Rovers	42	11	7	3	34	15	4	6	11	18	31	43
10	Newport County	42	15	4	2	39	15	2	5	14	17	49	43
11	Norwich City	42	13	5	3	45	18	3	3	15	15	41	40
12	Aberdare Athletic	42	9	9	3	35	18	3	5	13	10	40	38
13	Merthyr Town	42	11	8	2	33	19	0	8	13	12	46	38
14	Charlton Athletic	42	8	7	6	26	20	3	8	10	12	25	37
15	Gillingham	42	11	6	4	27	15	1	7	13	16	43	37
16	Exeter City	42	14	3	4	33	17	1	4	16	4	35	37
17	Brentford	42	9	8	4	33	21	5	0	16	21	50	36
18	Reading	42	12	2	7	35	20	1	7	13	16	37	35
19	Southend United	42	11	7	3	35	19	1	3	17	18	65	34
20	Watford	42	8	8	5	35	18	1	7	13	10	36	33
21	Bournemouth	42	6	8	7	19	19	5	3	13	21	46	33
22	QPR	42	9	6	6	28	26	2	3	16	9	51	31

Pompey player born on 18 March

Henry (Harry) Middleton b.1937

Pompey players born on 19 March

Anthony (Tony) John Priscott b.1941;
Roy Harold Smith b.1936;
Roy Donald Summersby b.1935;
Scott Peter Wilson b.1977

— STAR & CRESCENT HERO – GUY WHITTINGHAM —

Guy holds the club record for number of League goals scored in a season. He netted 42 League goals for Pompey in the 1992/93 season.

Guy started playing football for the army and was a late starter in the professional game, not signing for Pompey until he was 24 years old. Before coming to Pompey, he had experience of playing for Oxford City, Waterlooville and Yeovil, while still serving in the army.

He was signed by manager John Gregory in the summer of 1989, for a fee of £450 (the amount needed to buy himself out of the army). This has got to be one of the all-time bargains in Pompey's history. During his first season (1989/90), Guy managed to score 23 League goals in 39 appearances – not bad for someone who had not played professionally before.

The next two seasons were not quite so prolific for Guy, although he still managed to net 12 goals and 11 goals in the 1990/91 and 1991/92 seasons, respectively.

Then, in the summer of 1992, Darren Anderton moved to Tottenham, with Paul Walsh coming in the other direction. Whittingham formed a formidable partnership with Walsh, who was responsible for setting up a fair proportion of Guy's 47 goals in all competitions that season. The season ultimately ended in disappointment as Pompey missed out on promotion to the Premier League on goals scored to West Ham.

The summer saw Guy move on to Aston Villa where his career faltered somewhat, with his only managing five goals for the Villa. After spells with Wolves and Sheffield Wednesday, Guy returned to Fratton Park on loan in February 1999, in the club's hour of need. Scoring seven times in nine games, he helped pull off another one of Pompey's great escapes.

Late in 2000, Steve Claridge was appointed manager by then Chairman Milan Mandaric, and Steve called upon Guy, who was on loan at Oxford United at the time, to become his assistant. After four months in charge, Claridge was replaced by Graham Rix, and Guy was on the move again, this time to his final club Wycombe Wanderers, where he made an FA Cup semi-final appearance before hanging up his boots.

Pompey players born on 20 March

David (Dave) John Beasant b.1959;
Brian Bromley b.1946; James Peter Ellis b.1956;
Henry (Harry) Lunn b.1925;
Paul Charles Merson b.1968

— TRUE BLUE FACTS —

Bill Shankly's brother John played three matches and scored once for Pompey in the 1920s.

Guy Whittingham, who scored a club record 42 League goals in one season, failed to join the exclusive 100 Club when he stuck on 99 League goals.

Pompey's worst ever League result was a 10–0 defeat by Leicester City in 1928.

Pompey player born on 21 March
John Thomas (Tom) Cope b.1882

Pomp & Posterity – 1925–26
The New South Stand at Fratton Park was opened by John McKenna, the President of the Football League – it was 360ft long and cost £20,000

Pompey players born on 22 March
Carl James Petteer b.1981;
Matthew Michael (Matt 'Ginger') Reilly b.1874

— BEST EVER GATE TOP TEN —

1 =	Pompey	v	Derby	1949, 51,385
2 =	Pompey	v	Wolverhampton	1949, 50,248
3 =	Pompey	v	Manchester Utd	1950, 49,962
4 =	Pompey	v	Tottenham	1951, 49,716
5 =	Pompey	v	Newport	1949, 48,581
6 =	Pompey	v	Blackpool	1950, 47,829
7 =	Pompey	v	West Ham	1939, 47,614
8 =	Pompey	v	Liverpool	1950, 47,507
9 =	Pompey	v	Sheffield Weds	1949, 47,188
10 =	Pompey	v	Tottenham	1951, 46,815

Pompey player born on 23 March
Andrew (Andy) Peter b.1975

— TRUE BLUE FACTS —

Hearts were the first Scottish team to play at Fratton Park in 1926.

Three Pompey players were sent off in the same game by referee Kelvin Morton. Billy Gilbert, Mick Tait and Kevin Dillon were all shown the red card in a 1–0 league defeat away to Sheffield United in the 1986–87 season.

Kevin Dillon once scored a hat-trick of penalties in a Full Members Cup-tie 3–2 win against Millwall.

Pompey players born on 24 March
Martyn George Busby b.1953;
Aliou Cisse b.1976

1926–27 League Division Two

		P	W	D	L	F	A	W	D	L	F	A	Pts
1	Middlesbrough	42	18	2	1	78	23	9	6	6	44	37	62
2	**Pompey**	**42**	**14**	**4**	**3**	**58**	**17**	**9**	**4**	**8**	**29**	**32**	**54**
3	Manchester City	42	15	3	3	65	23	7	7	7	43	38	54
4	Chelsea	42	13	7	1	40	17	7	5	9	22	35	52
5	Nottingham Forest	42	14	6	1	57	23	4	8	9	23	32	50
6	Preston NE	42	14	4	3	54	29	6	5	10	20	43	49
7	Hull City	42	13	4	4	43	19	7	3	11	20	33	47
8	Port Vale	42	11	6	4	50	26	5	7	9	38	52	45
9	Blackpool	42	13	5	3	65	26	5	3	13	30	54	44
10	Oldham	42	12	3	6	50	37	7	3	11	24	47	44
11	Barnsley	42	13	5	3	56	23	4	4	13	32	64	43
12	Swansea City	42	13	5	3	44	21	3	6	12	24	51	43
13	S***hampton	42	9	8	4	35	22	6	4	11	25	40	42
14	Reading	42	14	1	6	47	20	2	7	12	17	52	40
15	Wolverhampton W	42	10	4	7	54	30	4	3	14	19	45	35
16	Notts Co	42	11	4	6	45	24	4	1	16	25	72	35
17	Grimsby Town	42	6	7	8	39	39	5	5	11	35	52	34
18	Fulham	42	11	4	6	39	31	2	4	15	19	61	34
19	Gateshead	42	10	8	3	49	25	1	3	17	22	71	33
20	Leyton Orient	42	9	3	9	37	35	3	4	14	23	61	31
21	Darlington	42	10	3	8	53	42	2	3	16	26	56	30
22	Bradford City	42	6	4	11	30	28	1	5	15	20	60	23

Pomp & Posterity – 1926–27

This season saw the arrival of top-flight football at Fratton Park when the club finished second in the League behind Middlesbrough, to secure an automatic promotion place. Pompey were not only the first Southern League club to gain promotion to the top division, but they were also the first club to climb up from the Third Division. After this achievement, McCartney resigned due to health issues and was replaced by John (Jack) Tinn.

Pompey player born on 25 March
Alfred George Abraham (Alf Dusty) Miller b.1917

Pompey players born on 26 March
Edward (Ted) Hewitt Platt b.1921; Alan Pringle b.1914; Thomas (Tommy) Cook Quigley b.1932

— WORST EVER GATE TOP TEN —

1 = Pompey	v	Bristol City	1993, 2,318
2 = Pompey	v	Lucchese	1992, 2,363
3 = Pompey	v	Wimbledon	1989, 2,499
4 = Pompey	v	Crystal Palace	1986, 2,515
5 = Pompey	v	Millwall	1992, 2,535
6 = Pompey	v	Hull City	1988, 2,784
7 = Pompey	v	Cosenza	1993, 2,961
8 = Pompey	v	Charlton	1985, 3,074
9 = Pompey	v	Blackpool	1992, 3,096
10 = Pompey	v	Stoke City	1987, 3,228

Pompey player born on 27 March
Stephen Charles (Steve) Smith b.1896

Pompey players born on 28 March
Stephen (Steve) Roy Middleton b.1953; Andrew (Andy) John Thomson b.1974

Pomp & Posterity – 1926–27

The opening match v Saints was watched by 27,896.
Pompey won 3–1.

Pompey player born on 29 March
Daniel (Dan) Cunliffe b.1875

— TRUE BLUE FACTS —

John 'Jock' Gilfillan played in the 1927 Scottish Cup for East Fife and for Pompey in the 1929 and 1934 Cup Finals, collecting runner-up medals on each occasion.

Pompey have made three FA Cup final appearances - 1929, 1934 and the one they won, 1939.

Pompey's first ever relegation came when they finished bottom, having won only six games during the season 1958–59.

— STAR & CRESCENT HERO - ANDY AWFORD —

Andy Awford had the distinction of being the youngest ever player to play for Pompey's first team when he made his debut against Crystal Palace at Selhurst Park in April 1989. At the age of 16, John Gregory felt Andy had what it takes and had no hesitation in giving him his chance, following injuries to Gavin Maguire and Graeme Hogg. After turning in an accomplished performance, he made another three appearances that season.

However, it wasn't until the 1991–92 season that Andy really made a name for himself. Jim Smith was now the manager and put his faith in several young and untested players such as Kit Symons, Darren Anderton, Chris Burns and Darryl Powell. Awford only missed one game that season, and at the age of 19 faced the likes of John Barnes and Ian Rush in the FA Cup semi-final against Liverpool.

Unfortunately, some fans may best remember Andy for the moment he committed the foul outside the Pompey box in the dying minutes that ultimately led to the Liverpool equaliser.

The following season saw Andy and Kit Symons form a youthful but extremely effective central defensive partnership, only conceding nine goals at Fratton Park all season. Once again, however, the season ended in heartache with Pompey missing out on promotion on goals scored to West Ham.

Early career promise was not fulfilled, however, as Awford suffered with injuries. The first and most serious coming at West Brom in September 1994, when he broke his leg. Andy's career never really recovered from this and, despite staying at Pompey, he retired from the game in November 2000 at the age of just 28.

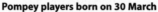

Pompey players born on 30 March
Eoin Kevin Joseph Colin Hand b.1946;
Christopher (Chris) John Price b.1960;
Gary Andrew Stevens b.1962

— MEMORABLE GAMES —

Pompey v Notts County (Fratton Park)
9 April 1927
Result: 9–1
Pompey goal scorers: Forward, Mackie (2), Haines (3), Davies, Cook (2)

This win saw Pompey register their record victory, and all but guaranteed them promotion to the First Division for the first time in their history. The 15,000-strong crowd witnessed a dominant Pompey performance.

The match was played in terrible conditions, with heavy rain falling throughout the game. However, the performance and result ensured that, although drenched, the crowd went home happy.

Pompey were off to a flyer with four goals coming in the first 22 minutes. However, by half-time County had pulled one back as the teams went in with the score at 4–1 to Pompey. The second half put the result beyond doubt, though, with a further five goals coming from Pompey. With Pompey's push for promotion, this was another valuable three points and an important increase in goal average.

Pompey player born on 31 March
James (Jim) Storrie b.1940

Pomp & Posterity – 1927–28

Pompey became the south of England's first Division One club.

Pompey found life difficult in their first season in the top flight. The club's second season brought mixed fortunes with an FA Cup Final appearance against Bolton Wanderers, while in the League they faced a relegation battle. This season also saw the worst defeat in the club's history.

Pompey player born on 1 April
Ian James Baird b.1964

— TRUE BLUE FACTS —

Goalkeeper John Jarvie was born in Old Monkland.

When Jimmy Allen went for a British transfer record of £10,775, the money was used to rebuild the North Stand, which is why it's sometimes called the Jimmy Allen Stand.

Pompey players born on 2 April
Eyal Berkovic b.1972;
Edward (Teddy) Paul Sheringham b.1966;
Alfred Henry (Alf) Strange b.1900;
Thomas Thogersen b.1968

— TO THE FRATTON FAITHFUL —

The better team won in the end, though our boys held them well and did not lack anything in skill; it was a pity Bell was injured for I think that incident was the turning point of the game.

Pompey's captain John McIlwaine after the 1929 FA Cup Final

Pompey player born on 3 April
Robert (Bob) Mortimar b.1908

Pompey player born on 4 April
Stephen (Steve) Andrew Berry b.1963

— TO THE FRATTON FAITHFUL —

The Football Mail *organised commentary of the game to be relayed back to Fratton Park, with the gates opening at 2pm. The crowd were entertained beforehand by community singing and band music.*

***The News* (reporting the Fratton Park 'beam back' of the 1929 FA Cup Final)**

Pompey player born on 5 April
John Edward (Eddie) Lever b.1911

— MEMORABLE GAMES —

1929 FA Cup Final – Pompey v Bolton Wanderers

Semi-finals, Saturday, 23 March 1929

Aston Villa 0–1 Pompey (Highbury, London)
Pompey goal scorer: Smith (penalty)

Bolton Wanderers 3–1 Huddersfield Town (Anfield, Liverpool)
Bolton goal scorers: Blackmore, Butler, Gibson
Huddersfield goal scorer: Jackson

Bolton were starting to be regulars at Wembley after their two previous FA Cup victories during the 1920s. The Trotters had beaten Oldham and Liverpool in the opening rounds and a rare goal from Jimmy Seddon helped the Wanderers to win 2–1 at Leicester in the 5th round. They had knocked out Blackburn Rovers, the holders, in the last eight, at Ewood Park, and over £500 worth of Wembley ticket applications had already been received at Burnden Park, such was the confidence of success. A crowd of 62,522 paid £4,722, a then attendance and receipt record for the ground, with a 2–2 draw resulting. The replay attracted Burnden Park's best midweek crowd of 65,295 – a record wasn't established due to poor packing in of the crowd. Two Billy Butler goals gave the Wanderers a 2–1 win. The other finalists of 1928 were defeated in the semi-finals.

Pompey had never been further than the last 32 in the Cup. Bolton concluded their season at 14th in the First Division, their worst position since the First World War. Portsmouth, who had been a First Division club for just two years, escaped relegation once more by the skin of their collective teeth, finishing 20th for the second consecutive year.

FA Cup Final (Wembley)
Pompey v Bolton Wanderers
27 April 1929
Result: 0–2
Referee: A Josephs (South Shields)
Attendance: 92,576

Bolton's experience helped them to control the match, but it took until the 78th minute for them to score. A penetrating attack by Billy Butler concluded with the winger shooting past Gilfillan and defender Mackie on the line. Wanderers' second came when Butler crossed for Harold Blackmore to blast it past the helpless keeper in the final minute of the game and give himself the record of scoring in every round of that season's Cup campaign.

Bolton Wanderers Dick Pym, Bob Haworth, Alex Finney, Fred Kean, Jimmy Seddon (Captain), Harry Nuttall, Billy Butler (Scorer), Jim McClelland, Harold Blackmore (Scorer), George Gibson, Willie Cook, Charles Foweraker (Manager)
Pompey John Gilfillan, Alex Mackie, Thomas Bell, Jimmy Nichol, Johnny McIlwaine, David Thackeray, Fred Forward, Jack Smith, John Weddle, David Watson, Fred Cook, Jack Tinn (Manager)

Pompey player born on 6 April
John (Sailor) Hunter b.1878

— STAR & CRESCENT HERO – JOHN WEDDLE —

John Weddle, a former miner, was signed by manager Jack Tinn in September 1927 at just 19 years of age, and proved to be a more than adequate replacement for the legendary Billy Haines.

Weddle was signed from Fatfield Albion, a colliery side that played near Sunderland, and the young man made an instant impression at Fratton Park. Although just 5ft 9in tall, his strength and direct play made him a feared centre-forward (of the old school) and, during his first 14 League appearances for Pompey, Weddle netted nine times. He finished off his first season with his new club by hitting four against S***hampton in the Hampshire Cup Final.

Some have compared him to former Pompey striker Guy Whittingham. Neither was tall or an overtly skilful player, but they both had the instinct to be in the right place at the right time. At the tender age of 21, John got his first taste of Wembley in the FA Cup Final, running out with Pompey to face the renowned Bolton Wanderers. In the programme for the match, he was said to be 'a thrusting leader of the Portsmouth attack who is fearless and persistent... He can hit a ball with great force and has worrying tactics likely to upset the Wanderers today'.

The diminutive player was to become one of Portsmouth's greatest goal scorers and was given the epithet 'Steamboat Weddle' by the Fratton crowd in recognition of his power and endeavour, and the fans on the north terrace could often be heard urging their team to 'Give it to Weddle!' during quiet periods in the course of play. He was a popular figure throughout the 1930s, scoring several hat-tricks along the way, his first coming against Burnley at Fratton Park in January 1930 in a 7–1 defeat of the Clarets. But perhaps his most famous 'haul of three' helped to knock Leicester City out of the 1934 FA

Cup at the semi-final stage, and sent Steamboat and his club to Wembley for a second time. That season was to be John's most successful period with Pompey – he netted 24 League goals in 39 appearances.

Weddle developed a probing combination with Willie Smith and Jimmy Easson and it is probably true to say that without these two accomplices John could not have achieved the glory of being Pompey's leading marksman in half-a-dozen seasons.

Steamboat was also an all-round sportsman, and would return to his native North East each summer to play cricket for Whitburn.

After spending over 10 years with Pompey, at the age of 30, Weddle had become Pompey's longest-serving player and highest-ever goal scorer. With 170 goals in 368 League appearances, he still holds the mantle of the club's all-time second-highest goal scorer.

John moved on to Blackburn Rovers, where he took on a coaching role. He remained at Ewood Park until 1958 when he retired from football. His name has become all but forgotten by present-day Pompey fans. However, today his talent would make him priceless. Steamboat Weddle passed away in 1979 aged 71.

Pompey players born on 7 April

Alexander (Sandy) Brown b.1879; Derek Gamblin b.1943;
Carl Basil Hayward b.1928; Oliver Albert George Ley b.1946;
James Baillie (Jimmy) Nichol b.1903;
William Gallacher (Tim) Williamson b.1900

Pompey player born on 8 April

Stephen Dearm b.1900

POMPEY PUB

Mr Pickwick
Milton Road, Milton

Pompey player born on 9 April

Michael (Mick) Francis Martin Kennedy b.1961

Pomp & Posterity – 1930–31

Fratton Park returfed.

Pompey player born on 10 April

Stephen (Steve) Edward Claridge b.1966

— TO THE FRATTON FAITHFUL —

Saturday, 1 March 1930

Pompey's playing kit was destroyed in a drying-room fire. Manager Jack Tinn and other players extinguished the fire before the brigade arrived. Pompey had to play their friendly game in salmon-pink jerseys.

Pompey players born on 11 April

Thomas G (Tommy) Bell b.1899; James (Jimmy) Charles Campbell b.1937; John (Jack) Shufflebotham b.1885

— MEMORABLE GAMES —

1934 FA Cup Final – Pompey v Manchester City

Semi-finals, Saturday, 17 March 1934

Aston Villa 1–6 Manchester City (Leeds Road, Huddersfield)
Villa goal scorer: Astley
City goal scorers: Toseland, Tilson (4), Herd

Leicester City 1–4 Pompey (St Andrew's, Birmingham)
Leicester goal scorer: Lochead
Pompey goal scorers: Weddle (3), Rutherford

A remarkable Cup run in 1933/34 captivated the city. Manchester United were beaten 4–1 and Bolton Wanderers 3–0, amongst others, before Leicester 4–1 and a John Weddle hat-trick against Birmingham in the semi-final took Pompey to Wembley to meet Manchester City.

FA Cup Final (Wembley)
Pompey v Manchester City
28 April 1934
Result: 1–2
Pompey goal scorer: Rutherford
Referee: S Rous (Watford)
Attendance: 93,258

City returned to Wembley determined to make amends for their performance in the 1933 final. They had finished 5th in the First Division, a big improvement on the previous two seasons. Pompey finished 10th. City arrived confident having put six past Aston Villa in the previous round.

Pompey were back at Wembley again, some five years after their last appearance.

In the 27th minute, Weddle sent Sep Rutherford away down the left. He cut inside, and fired past Swift to give Pompey the lead. Pompey held it until 16 minutes from the end, when Jimmy Allen, the Pompey captain, went off injured. City seized their chance. Brook set off on a mazy run and passed to star centre-forward Fred Tilson; the striker, who had netted four times in the semi-final, shot past Gilfillan for the equaliser. With the game heading for extra-time, Herd's pass enabled Tilson to score again with four minutes left. Some argued that, if it wasn't for the injury to Pompey's stalwart Allen, they would have gone on to win comfortably. He had been a passenger for long periods, after Pompey had taken the lead.

The referee was Stanley Rous, who would go on to become pre-eminent in football both in England and around the world. His contribution was recognised when he had the World Cup named after him.

Months after the final at Wembley, centre-half Jim Allen was transferred to Aston Villa for a then British record fee of £10,775. The money was used to finance major development at Fratton Park, including building a new North Stand, which stands to this day, and increased the capacity to 58,000.

Manchester City Frank Swift, Laurie Barnett, Billy Dale, (Sir) Matt Busby, Sam Cowan (Captain), Jackie Bray, Ernie Toseland, Bobby Marshall, Fred Tilson (Scored 2), Alec Herd, Eric Brook, Wilf Wild (Manager)

Pompey John Gilfillan, Alex Mackie, Billy Smith, Jimmy Nichol, Jim Allen (Captain), David Thackeray, Fred Worrall, Jack Smith, John Weddle, Jim Easson, Sep Rutherford (Scorer), Jack Tinn (Manager)

Pompey players born on 12 April

Stuart Dunbar Croft b.1954;
John George Lathan b.1952;
Alexander (Alex) McDonald b.1878;
Charles (Charlie) Thomas Reginald Mortimore b.1928;
Brian Geoffrey Yeo b.1944

Pompey players born on 13 April

Leonardo (Leo) Angel Biagini b.1977;
Gerrard (Gerry) Thomas Creaney b.1970;
Fred Edward Didymus b.1896;
Mervyn John Gill b.1931

— TO THE FRATTON FAITHFUL —

Before the 1934 FA Cup Final

Music-hall star Bud Flanagan visited Pompey's changing room, although the morale-boosting trick didn't work. Bud Flanagan was a popular wartime entertainer. He was best known as part of double act Flanagan and Allen, with Chesney Allen. As music-hall comedians, they would often feature a mixture of comedy and music in their act and this led to a successful recording career as a duo and roles in film and television. Flanagan and Allen were also both members of The Crazy Gang and worked with that team for many years concurrently with their double-act career.

— TO THE FRATTON FAITHFUL —

All I remember is the Cup Final.

Anonymous Pompey fan arrested for drunkenness and disorderly conduct in Landport, after the 1934 FA Cup Final

Pompey player born on 14 April
Louis Noe Pamarot b.1979

— STAR & CRESCENT HERO – JIMMY EASSON —

Scotland's Jimmy Easson scored over 100 League goals for Pompey; he was one of just three players to achieve that milestone before the Second World War.

Although diminutive and fragile looking, Jimmy was amongst some of the most feared inside-forwards in the First Division before the Second World War.

Born in the neat little city of Brechin, Easson started his footballing career with Dundee. Pompey's manager Jack Tinn persuaded Jim to cross the border in 1928 and his first match in the English top flight took him to Old Trafford in 1929, following Pompey's FA Cup final disappointment. The debutant put on a creditable display in a 0–0 draw. Jim struck twice against local rivals S***hampton in the Pickford Benevolent Cup a few days later.

Easson won a regular place in the first team when he replaced David Watson. He was quick to demonstrate his knack for finding the net, hitting five goals in his first 10 matches.

Jimmy's reputation spread during the 1930–31 term when in the space of a month he scored two Fratton Park hat-tricks, against Manchester United and

Liverpool. Not long after this, he was selected to play for England, but the offer was quickly withdrawn when it was realised the man was no Sassenach. However, Jim was to win three Scottish caps.

Easson concluded the 1930–31 season with 30 League and Cup goals to help Pompey finish fourth in the First Division. With Jimmy and his teammate John Weddle, who scored 24 goals, Pompey had a strike partnership that caused trepidation throughout the English game at the start of the 1930s.

In the 1931–32 season, Easson struck another hat-trick, missed just a couple of games and achieved a goal tally of 21. It was not unusual for the 'Wee Man' to bag a brace in a match and he became a Fratton Park favourite.

Jim played in the FA Cup Final win over Manchester City in 1934. In December 1938, his final game in the royal blue ended in the same way as his debut for the club; against Manchester United, it was a 0–0 draw. In 1939, Jim moved to Craven Cottage.

Only a handful of players in the chronicles of Portsmouth FC have scored more goals than Jimmy Easson. He remains one of Pompey's greatest marksman, having hit 102 goals in 294 appearances.

Pompey player born on 15 April

Craig Andrew Foster b.1969

— POMPEY XIs – 'SONS' —

The following 11 players all have their surname end in 'son':

Name	Played
John 'Jock' Anderson	1933–39
Roger Davidson	1969–70
Jackie Henderson	1951–58
George Hudson	1947–48
William Morrison	1958–60
William Williamson	1924–25
Robert Widdowson	1969
John Robertson	1921–23
Ernest Thompson	1920–21
David Thompson	2006–present
Glen Johnson	2006–present

Pompey players born on 16 April

David Paul Birmingham b.1981; Isaac Tomlinson b.1880; Arjan De Zeeuw b.1970

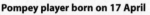

Pompey player born on 17 April
James (Jimmy) McLean McIlwraith b.1954

Pomp & Posterity – 1930–36

1930/31 – Pompey finished in 4th position. Jimmy Allen had been installed at centre-half; Freddie Worrall, from Oldham, had replaced Freddie Forward on the wing and Weddle had formed a good partnership with new signing Jimmy Easson, which brought them 20 goals each in the following season.

1935/36 – Portsmouth failed to arrive for their League match at Brentford and the match was postponed.

Pompey player born on 18 April
William Moses Edwards b.1893

— TRUE BLUE FACTS —

Pompey not only reached the FA Cup Final once again in the 1938/39 season, but were also victors over favourites Wolverhampton Wanderers, winning 4–1.

Somehow, Fratton Park suffered no bomb damage during the war, despite Portsmouth being heavily bombed.

1946 was the first season after the Second World War and much was in short supply due to rationing. Pompey fans donated their clothing coupons to enable Pompey to buy royal-blue shirts to play in.

Pompey player born on 19 April
Harry Digweed b.1878

Pompey players born on 20 April
Nicos Kyzeridis b.1971;
Alan Francis McLoughlin b.1967;
Laurence (Laurie) Courtney Milligan b.1958

— TRUE BLUE FACTS —

In 1936 Pompey reserves won the London Combination League.

Lindy Delapenha was Pompey's winger in the 1948/49 and 1949/50 seasons, playing seven League games and scoring on his only FA Cup appearance.

Pompey player born on 21 April
Joseph Charles (Joe) Dix b.1886

1938–39 League Division One

		P	W	D	L	F	A	W	D	L	F	A	Pts
1	Everton	42	17	3	1	60	18	10	2	9	28	34	59
2	Wolverhampton W	42	14	6	1	55	12	8	5	8	33	27	55
3	Charlton Athletic	42	16	3	2	49	24	6	3	12	26	35	50
4	Middlesbrough	42	13	6	2	64	27	7	3	11	29	47	49
5	Arsenal	42	14	3	4	34	14	5	6	10	21	27	47
6	Derby County	42	12	3	6	39	22	7	5	9	27	33	46
7	Stoke City	42	13	6	2	50	25	4	6	11	21	43	46
8	Bolton W	42	10	6	5	39	25	5	9	7	28	33	45
9	Preston NE	42	13	7	1	44	19	3	5	13	19	40	44
10	Grimsby Town	42	11	6	4	38	26	5	5	11	23	43	43
11	Liverpool	42	12	6	3	40	24	2	8	11	22	39	42
12	Aston Villa	42	11	3	7	44	25	5	6	10	27	35	41
13	Leeds Utd	42	11	5	5	40	27	5	4	12	19	40	41
14	Manchester Utd	42	7	9	5	30	20	4	7	10	27	45	38
15	Blackpool	42	9	8	4	37	26	3	6	12	19	42	38
16	Sunderland	42	7	7	7	30	29	6	5	10	24	38	38
17	**Pompey**	**42**	**10**	**7**	**4**	**25**	**15**	**2**	**6**	**13**	**22**	**55**	**37**
18	Brentford	42	11	2	8	30	27	3	6	12	23	47	36
19	Huddersfield Town	42	11	4	6	38	18	1	7	13	20	46	35
20	Chelsea	42	10	5	6	43	29	2	4	15	21	51	33
21	Birmingham City	42	10	5	6	40	27	2	3	16	22	57	32
22	Leicester City	42	7	6	8	35	35	2	5	14	13	47	29

Pompey players born on 22 April
William Alexander Clark Beedie b.1894;
Scott Thomas McGarvey b.1963; Darren Mark Moore b.1974;
Lee Robert Sandford b.1968; Stephen (Steve) Soley b.1971

Pompey players born on 23 April
Philip (Phil) William Rookes b.1919;
Charles (Charlie) John Vaughn b.1921

— TO THE FRATTON FAITHFUL —

Portsmouth are a lucky side because they have 11 good players, a good trainer, a good manager, good directors and a Lord Bishop to travel with them and bring them luck.

The Lord Bishop of Portsmouth following the 1939 Cup Final

Pompey players born on 24 April
Robert (Bobby) Campbell b.1937;
James (Jimmy) William Dickinson b.1925

— MEMORABLE GAMES —

1939 FA Cup Final – Wolverhampton Wanderers v Pompey

Semi-finals, Saturday, 25 March 1939

Grimsby Town 0–5 Wolves (Old Trafford
Grimsby goal scorers: Westcott (4), Galley (penalty)

Huddersfield Town 1–2 Pompey (Highbury)
Huddersfield goal scorer: Barclay
Pompey goal scorers: Barlow, Anderson

Pompey were hoping to take the FA Cup to the south coast for the first time. Comfortable home wins against Lincoln, West Bromwich Albion and West Ham United led to a quarter-final meeting with Preston North End. The Lilywhites, the holders, were eliminated and Pompey were set to meet the other finalists of 1938. After going behind at Highbury, it took two late goals from Bert Barlow and Jock Anderson to take them through to their third final.

Wolves had won the Cup twice previously, but the last occasion was in 1908, when they defeated Newcastle United 3–1 in the Crystal Palace final. The last of their five previous finals had been in 1921, when they were beaten 1–0 by Tottenham Hotspur at Stamford Bridge.

Pompey were a struggling First Division side, having finished 17th that season. Wolves concluded their schedule as League runners-up for the second year running to Everton, despite trouncing the Toffees 7–0 in a League match, and knocking them out of the Cup in the quarter-finals.

Wolverhampton Wanderers were a highly rated team. The respective League positions of the two clubs ensured Wolves were firm favourites. The much fancied Wolves side contain household names such as Cullis, whereas Pompey were the widest outsiders in Cup Final history, and the whole country expected the Midlanders to find consolation at Wembley for missing out on the League title. But the boys from Fratton Park put their faith in the legendary 'lucky spats', worn by manager Jack Tinn at every Cup match that season, and looked forward to them working their accustomed magic.

FA Cup Final (Wembley)
Wolverhampton Wanderers v Pompey
29 April 1939
Result: 1–4
Pompey goal scorers: Anderson, Barlow, Parker (2)
Referee: T Thompson (Leamington-on-Tyne)
Attendance: 99,370

The burden of being overwhelming favourites made Wolves look nervous but the occasion did not seem to affect Pompey, as they turned in a brilliant display. With 31 minutes gone, Bert Barlow, signed from Wolves only two months earlier, took a pass from Anderson and struck a great shot past Scott into the corner. A minute before half-time, the Pompey Chimes were ringing out loudly around Wembley, after Jock Anderson, having collected Worrall's high cross, went past Cullis to shoot. Scott got his hands to the ball but only succeeded in pushing it into the top of the net.

A minute into the second half, the volume was raised further. Scott initially saved from Barlow, but the ball squirmed out of his grasp. He managed to recover, and stopped it, with one hand, on the line. Unfortunately for him, Cliff Parker ran in and knocked the ball in before the keeper could get his other hand on it.

Wolves struck back when Westcott put Dickie Dorsett through to score, but they were never really in the game, and Parker completed the scoring with his second, a header from another Worrall cross.

Pompey had been superb and had swept the young Wolves aside with a magnificent display.

James 'Jimmy' Guthrie had the honour of lifting the FA Cup for the first time in the history of Portsmouth FC. But as he took the trophy from His Majesty King George VI he was ready to give credit to heroes such as Tommy Rowe at centre-half, Guy Wharton partnering Guthrie at half-back, inside-forwards Bert Barlow and Jimmy McAlinden and the emerging Jock Anderson at centre-forward.

The Pompey players and officials caught the train back to Fratton station where they were met by thousands of adoring fans.

S***hampton played at the Dell on the same day in front of just 4,000 fans, as it was rumoured many of their supporters made the trip to Wembley to cheer on their south-coast neighbours. How times have changed!

Pompey George Walker, Lew Morgan, Bill Rochford, Jimmy Guthrie (Captain), Tommy Rowe, Guy Wharton, Fred Worrall, Jimmy McAlinden, Jock Anderson (Scorer), Bert Barlow (Scorer), Cliff Parker (Scored 2), Jack Tinn (Manager)
Wolverhampton Wanderers Robert Scott, Billy Morris, Jack Taylor, Tom Galley, Stan Cullis (Captain), Joe Gardiner, Stan Burton, Alex McIntosh, Dennis Westcott, Dickie Dorsett (Scorer), Teddy Maguire, Frank Buckley (Manager)

Pompey player born on 25 April
C B Fry b.1872

Pompey player born on 26 April
Michael Dowling b.1889

— STAR & CRESCENT HERO – JIMMY GUTHRIE —

Born in Perth in 1912, Jimmy Guthrie was the skipper of the Pompey side that won the FA Cup in April 1939. Wolves were subjected to a shock 4–1 defeat that rated as the most unexpected result seen up to that point at that proud stadium.

Guthrie, then 27 years old and playing right-half, contributed some tough tackling and fine leadership. Looking back many years on, he commented, 'You can get away with murder in the first 10 minutes of a Cup Final.'

Jimmy was part of the Scottish footballing exodus that flooded into England after the Second World War and signed for Pompey for £4,000 (a considerable fee in 1937) from Dundee, as a 25-year-old (he was much later to admit to receiving an illegal bonus of £600 when he joined Pompey). Soon after, he was joined at Fratton Park by Guy Wharton and Bert Barlow and, supported by Lou Morgan, Bill Rochford and Tommy Rowe in defence and Harry Walker in goal, Guthrie's poise and assurance developed.

Jimmy took on the role of the Players' Union representative and became a popular personality. But, unfortunately, the 1939 FA Cup final was his last first-team game of any importance. Like innumerable players of his generation, his career was destroyed with the outbreak of war.

In July 1939, following a car accident, Jimmy fought for his life in a Yorkshire hospital. He recovered in time to see the opening of the 1939–40 season, but after just three matches had been played war was declared.

Guthrie was to return to football, turning out for Pompey during the war years including another Wembley appearance in the War Cup Final of 1942 when Pompey were defeated by Brentford (2–0).

Jimmy was 34 on the cessation of hostilities, which at that time was too old for Division One football. After 76 games for Pompey (he scored two goals), he joined Crystal Palace in the Third Division South as player-coach and went on to spend a short period with Guildford in the Southern League.

Guthrie's final career was as a leading sportswriter with the *Sunday People*. He died in September 1981 at the age 68.

Pompey players born on 27 April
Robert (Rob) Hindmarsh b.1961;
Albert Edward (Kelly) Houlker

Pompey player born on 28 April
Edward George (Ted) Watson b.1885

Pomp & Posterity – 1939

Freddie Worrall appeared at a Wembley final three times, twice with Pompey in 1934 and 1939 and in the 1950s as the trainer of Warrington Rugby League Club.

Pompey players born on 29 April
Robert William (Bobby) Irvine b.1900;
David Munks b.1947

— TRUE BLUE FACT —

Pompey have never lost to a non-League club in the FA Cup, a feat shared with West Ham United and Leeds United.

Pompey player born on 30 April
Lewis (Lew) Morgan b.1911

Pompey player born on 1 May
Alexei Smertin b.1975

POMPEY PUB
The Devonshire Arms
Devonshire Avenue, Southsea

Pompey players born on 2 May
Michael (Mick) Quinn b.1962;
Leonard Stanley (Len) Williams b.1910

Pompey player born on 3 May
Albert Victor Walker b.1902

Pomp & Posterity – September–October 1939

With the outbreak of the Second World War, League fixtures were suspended. The FA Cup was placed in the basement of the Guildhall until 1945.

Pompey player born on 4 May
Duncan Gilchrist b.1903

Pompey player born on 5 May
Thomas (Tom) Gray b.1891

— TO THE FRATTON FAITHFUL —

In away games as in all other games start level.

Bob Jackson

Pompey player born on 6 May
Ronald (Ron) Rafferty b.1934

Pompey player born on 7 May
John Robert (Jack) Bainbridge b.1880

Pompey players born on 8 May
John (Jock) Curr Anderson b.1915;
Ronald (Ron) Bennett b.1927;
George Edward Pateman b.1910

Pompey players born on 9 May
William (Bill) Mark Atkins b.1939;
Trevor Lee Roberts b.1961;
James Scotland (Scot) Symon b.1911;
James Hunter (Jimmy) Thomson b.1884

— TRUE BLUE FACT —

The last time Pompey beat Chelsea was when Jimmy White scored in a 1–0 victory at Fratton Park back on 14 December 1960, some 46 years ago. Since then, Pompey have failed to beat the Londoners on 19 attempts.

Pompey player born on 10 May
Thomas (Tommy) Edward McGhee b.1929

Pompey player born on 11 May
Bernard Lambourde b.1971

— TRUE BLUE FACT —

Duggie 'Thunderboots' Reid had a shot so fierce it actually broke the net at the Milton End in the game against Manchester City in 1949. An even more devastating shot broke the net and even managed to bend a crash barrier behind the goal during an away match.

Pompey players born on 12 May
Albert Edward Mundy b.1926; Charles Martin Reagan b.1924

Pompey player born on 13 May
John Cumming b.1900

— STAR & CRESCENT HERO – DUGGIE REID —

Born in Mauchline, Scotland, on 3 October 1917, Duggie Reid was signed by Pompey manager Jack Tinn from Stockport County for £7,500 (a club record) in March 1946; he was 28 years old. It was something of a turn-up for the Scotsman, as the Second World War had robbed Reid of seven seasons and many considered that he'd lost the opportunity of playing at the highest level. But Pompey had watched him play 35 games for County in the War League and gave him his chance.

John Douglas Jamieson Reid had moved to the Manchester area with his family as a 15-year-old to take a job as an apprentice plumber. But he stood out in local amateur football and was spotted by Stockport County playing for local amateur team Heaton Chapel. He played 'A' team and reserve football for County from the age of 16 and signed professional forms with the Hatters in 1936. Duggie had made his first-team debut for Stockport on 3 October 1936 at the age of 19, winning two penalties in a 4–1 win over Oldham Athletic and played a small but significant role (10 appearances and three goals) in helping the club win the Third Division North title after defeating Lincoln City on the final day of the season in front of more than 27,000 rapturous supporters at Edgeley Park. He played at wing-half as the Edgeley Park club was relegated the following season.

Nicknamed 'Thunderboots' in celebration of his tremendous shooting ability, Duggie was a busy six-foot striker who was one of Pompey's most prolific post-war goal-getters and shone as one of the best marksmen in the Football League from 1946 to 1952. As such, it is a mystery why this Ayrshire hero never won an international cap for Scotland.

After signing for Pompey, Duggie had to ask Tinn where Portsmouth was – he had never travelled south of the Midlands. The supporters were somewhat wary when the gangly-looking young Reid arrived. But, when they saw him banging in the goals and witnessed the fierce and uncompromising penalties he smashed past opposing keepers, he became a great favourite with the Fratton Park faithful, playing in every match in his first full season and finishing with 29 goals, making him the club's leading goal scorer that term. He was to be Pompey's top marksman in four of the next five seasons and, at one point, Duggie had hit 120 goals in 222 games.

Regardless of his popularity, Duggie was a very diffident character; he avoided publicity and the adulation his ability attracted. The raw power let loose in his shot and his muscular presence was respected and feared by keepers throughout football and more than a few would quake as Thunderboots broke through their defences. Bert Williams, the keeper of the all-conquering 1950s

Wolves team and 24-times England international, was once asked by a journalist about the power of Duggie's drives. Actions spoke louder than words for Williams when he hoisted his jersey to expose a huge and angry contusion, etched by the match ball's panels, like the work of some manic, blind tattooist!

It seems that Duggie's credentials as a 'cannon-foot' were established early on in his career. Billy Titterington, a teammate and mentor of Reid's when he was with Stockport, recalled, 'We were playing away, maybe at Mansfield, and we won a free-kick 25 yards from goal. I moved wide to take an opponent with me and I said to him, "There's no need to come back and mark me."

'"What do you mean?" he replied.

'"Well, as soon as that lad hits the ball it will be in the back of the net. Your goalie will never see it."'

Billy's prediction came true.

One of the Pompey team that won League Championships in 1949 and 1950, Reid combined brilliantly with Peter Harris on the wing and together they formed an awesome strikeforce. His gangling gait could be misleading as he showed consistent and intelligent distribution skills; Duggie wasn't just a scorer and probably created as many goals as he netted himself.

In the latter part of his time at Fratton, Duggie converted to centre-half, filling the boots of Jack Froggatt, and proved a redoubtable defender, showing the same bravery he had exhibited during his days as a striker. But, like the esteemed Jimmy Dickinson, Reid was a gentleman on and off the field and never cheated.

Duggie bagged eight hat-tricks for Pompey, three against Chelsea in different seasons. However, perhaps his most memorable game was the last match of the 1949–50 campaign against Aston Villa. Pompey retained the Championship with a 5–1 victory. Duggie finished the season having scored 16 times in 27 League appearances. Reid was a first-class header of the ball and many of his goals were scored with his head as the boots and studs whisked around his ears; he'd often sustain vicious gashes to his head but always continued to head the ball without hesitation.

When Pompey keeper Ted Platt was injured, Reid went between the posts for 75 minutes in an FA Cup tie at Scunthorpe in January 1954. It appears he did well enough, as his side returned south having held the home team to a 1–1 draw.

Having scored 129 goals in 309 League games for Pompey, at the age of 38 after 10 seasons with Pompey, Duggie become player/manager at Tonbridge (although he continued to train at Fratton Park). However, after a year, the Pompey directors invited him to come back to the fold and run the club's new training ground and hostel at Tamworth Road, Copnor. In 1959, Reid was made head groundsman and he nurtured the Fratton Park pitch for two decades. In May 1980, Pompey played a testimonial game against S***hampton for Duggie in recognition of the quality and longevity of his service to the club, the high standard of the pitch being a testament to his dedication.

Duggie retired to his garden in Widley. He passed away on the morning of 8 February 2002; this was a day short of the 68th anniversary of his arrival as a Stockport County player. He will always be remembered as the 'Gentle Giant' and a lovely man.

Pompey player born on 14 May
Franck Songo'o b.1987

Pompey player born on 15 May
James F (Jimmy) Beattue b.1916

Pompey player born on 16 May
David (Dave) Graham Waterman b.1977

Pomp & Posterity – Post-World War II

League football returned shortly after the Second World War and the 1940s saw the introduction of future Pompey legends: Jimmy Dickinson, Jimmy Scoular, Len Phillips, Jack Froggatt, Peter Harris and Duggie Reid.

There was also a change in management at this time when Bob Jackson replaced Jack Tinn.

Pompey player born on 17 May
John Thomas (Tommy) Hakin b.1882

Pompey players born on 18 May
Dennis James Davidson b.1937;
Raymond (Ray) Drinkwater b.1931;
Barry Horne b.1962;
Gary Paul O'Neil b.1983

Pompey player born on 19 May
James Hall b.1915

Pompey players born on 20 May
Lloyd Lindbergh (Lindy) Delapenha b.1927;
Frederick (Fred) John Evans b.1923;
Henry (Harry) Ferrier b.1920;
George Henry (Harry) Walker b.1916

Pompey player born on 21 May
George Barnes b.1878

— STAR & CRESCENT HERO – JACK FROGGATT —

One of the finest players ever to have worn the royal blue of Pompey, Sheffield-born winger 'Jolly Jack' was a stocky, adventurous player whose powerful running and precise shooting brought recognition from the England selectors late in 1949 and he scored on his debut for his country at Maine Road, playing outside-left in a 9–2 demolition of Northern Ireland.

Alongside the redoubtable Scoular and Dickinson, Jack later formed the most commanding half-back line in football during the immediate post-war period, and these three formed the engine room of Pompey's successive First Division title-winning side.

Although he had played for the RAF, Froggatt started his football career at Fratton Park in 1945 while he was still in the service of his country. He had worked in his father's butchers shop but signed for Pompey as a centre-half. However, he quickly moved to outside-left.

The Froggatt family had firm connections with football. His father had been a Sheffield Wednesday pro before the war, while his second cousin Redfern Froggatt was to play 434 games for Wednesday.

On his debut for Pompey in the War League South at the Dell on 15 September 1945, Jack scored a second-half goal.

Jack possessed phenomenal speed and fine ball control. He was also strong in the air, and as such he became one of the most versatile players to wear the star and crescent over his heart.

On 6 April 1949, Jack scored a hat-trick of headers in a 5–0 away win at St James' Park in front of 60,000 Geordie fans. This was a glorious moment in Pompey's run-in to the Championship.

Froggatt's scoring and talented agility between 1949 and 1953 won him the distinction of playing for his country in three different positions. He scored twice in the process of winning 13 caps. When the swashbuckling winger transformed into a formidable centre-half, very few opponents got beyond big Jack.

In his final season as a Pompey player, Froggatt returned to the wing (Duggie Reid took over the No. 5 shirt).

Reluctantly, after 280 games in the blue and 66 goals to his credit, Jack left Pompey in March 1945 to join Leicester City. He played 143 games for the Foxes, finding the net on 18 occasions.

After leaving Filbert Street, Jack singed for Kettering. He eventually took over as player/manager of the club. His first game in sole charge was a home fixture against Yeovil Town on 18 January 1958. The Poppies thrashed the visitors 6–0. By the end of the season, Kettering had tasted defeat in just three League matches under the leadership of Jolly Jack and finished a respectable eighth in the Southern League.

The summer of 1958 saw the addition of a running track around the Rockingham Road pitch to allow the players to improve their fitness during training under the watchful eye of Froggatt.

At the conclusion of the 1958–59 season, Kettering finished as runners-up to Hereford United in the Southern League North – Western Zone and so qualified as founder members of the Premier Division of the Southern League. However, the Poppies were relegated to the Southern League First Division for the start of the 1960–61 season.

At the start of the 1961–62 campaign, Froggatt stepped down as Kettering manager, but stayed on at Rockingham Road to continue his playing career for another two seasons, before finally retiring in May 1963.

The former England and Pompey man is remembered at Kettering for his obdurate and inspiring leadership. His sleeves rolled up, he was a centre-half who was always in the thick of the battle and giving everything he had for the club cause.

On leaving Leicester and in tandem with his career with Kettering, Jack returned to Pompey as a publican, a career that would take up 22 years of his life. He was Mein Host at the Manor House in Cosham, the Milton Arms near Fratton Park and a hotel in Partridge Green, West Sussex.

JACK FROGGATT – ENGLAND RECORD

Type	Caps	Goals	Minutes played
Friendly	8	0	720
WC Qualifiers	1	1	90
Home Championships	4	1	360
Competitive	5	2	450
Total	**18**	**2**	**1170**

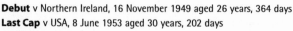

Debut v Northern Ireland, 16 November 1949 aged 26 years, 364 days
Last Cap v USA, 8 June 1953 aged 30 years, 202 days
Career 3 years, 203 days
First Goal v N Ireland, 16 November 1949 aged 26 years, 364 days

Starts 13
Substitute 0
Replaced 0
Full Games 13
08 Jun 53 v USA
18 Apr 53 v Scotland
26 Nov 52 v Belgium
12 Nov 52 v Wales (1)
04 Oct 52 v N Ireland
28 May 52 v Switzerland
25 May 52 v Austria
18 May 52 v Italy
05 Apr 52 v Scotland
28 Nov 51 v Austria
14 Apr 51 v Scotland
30 Nov 49 v Italy
16 Nov 49 v N Ireland (1)

— TRUE BLUE FACTS —

Tommy Rowe was awarded the DFC in 1943 but was shot down in March 1944 and spent the rest of the war as a POW.

From the 1990/91 season to 1999/2000, Pompey managed to win away only 49 out of 230 League matches. 1998/1999 was particularly bad with Pompey winning just once... at Port Vale!

Pompey players born on 22 May
Paul Mariner b.1953; Paul Moran b.1968

Pompey players born on 23 May
Aidan Robert Newhouse b.1972;
William (Bill) Rochford b.1913

Pomp & Posterity – 1944

Field Marshal Montgomery of Alamein elected President of Portsmouth FC.

Pompey player born on 24 May

Frederick J (Fred) Haycock b.1886

— TO THE FRATTON FAITHFUL —

The deeper the afternoon descended into farce, the longer they sang. It must have been the only time in football history that the supporters of a team being hammered by six goals were mocking the supporters of the team beating them!

The News **– Pompey, in Brazilian kit, lose 6–0 to Barnsley, 1999**

Pompey player born on 25 May

Isaac George (Pompey) Martin b.1889

Pompey player born on 26 May

Francis William (Frank) Hill b.1910

— TRUE BLUE FACT —

During the Second World War, Fratton Park's capacity was restricted to just 8,000.

Pompey players born on 27 May

Arthur T Foxall b.1897;

Lee Stuart Sharpe b.1971

Pompey player born on 28 May

Joseph S (Joe) Hisbent b.1882

— THE CREST —

Pompey's club crest, like its popular epithet, is taken from that of the city's. The official emblem is made up of a gold star and a crescent on a blue shield. Pompey's adoption of the star and crescent (traditionally associated with Islam) is said to have come from when King Richard I granted the city a crescent of gold on a shade of azure, with a blazing star of eight points.

The King had taken this from the Emperor's standard of Governor Isaac Komnenos, following the capture of Cyprus. It is amongst some of the most recognisable football crests in the English game and is nicknamed 'the smiley crest' because it looks a bit like a smiling face.

Throughout history, Pompey have developed variations of the crest but have always reverted to the basic gold star and crescent. In the 1950s and 1960s, the traditional crest was mounted on the shirt in white rather than gold but this was because white was a cheaper alternative.

Between 1980 and 1989, the original crest was replaced with a new design which showed a football on top of an anchor (representing the navy) and a sword (representing the army). An interchangeable version included a circular version of the star and crescent crest in place of the football.

The return of the original crest in 1989 lasted just four years before it was replaced by the city's coat of arms in 1993. This design centred on the basic star and crescent but it was unpopular with supporters who thought it was overly elaborate. After four seasons, the original crest was again reinstated and remains to the present day.

Pompey player born on 29 May

John (Jock) Hunter b.1875

Pompey players born on 30 May

Konstantinos Chalkias b.1974;
Robert (Bob) Michael Ridley b.1942;
James (Jim) Alfred Standen b.1935

Pomp & Posterity – 1946

Duggie Reid and Harry Ferrier joined Pompey.

Pompey player born on 31 May

William E (Billy) James b.1892

Pompey player born on 1 June

Bert A Youtman b.1893

— STAR & CRESCENT HERO – SASHA GAYDAMAK —

2006 saw the arrival of 29-year-old Alexandre (Sasha) Gaydamak at Pompey. He initially purchased half the club from then Chairman Milan Mandaric in January, and completed the full purchase later in the year.

Sasha grew up in France and Israel but is of Russian descent. His father, Arcadi, owns a football club in Israel. After studying economics in France, Sasha moved to London at the age of 20 and made a fortune in the City.

Now that he is the owner of Portsmouth Football Club, fans are hoping for a bright future with talk of significant investment in players and a new stadium.

Pompey players born on 2 June

Robert Roberts Taylor Blyth b.1900; Sebastien Schemmel b.1975

— A QUESTION FOR THE DEFENCE —

The nastiest, dirtiest player I have ever played against. He used to punch you, kick you, spit at you off the ball and he was an absolute nightmare.

Paul Walsh stating why Briggs of Oxford was his toughest opponent

Frank Burrows came in after the game with a piece of rope and said, 'Here, hang yourself with this.'

Billy Wilson after his two howlers against Grimsby was highlighted on *Match of the Day* over and over again

Eoin Hand gave away the penalty and we were out. A few Forest and Pompey fans ended the match in the River Trent that day! Great Cup run though.

Pompey defender Billy Wilson

Pompey players born on 3 June

Paul Anthony Hall b.1972; Alan Edward Knight b.1961; Terence (Terry) Roy Ryder b.1928

Pompey player born on 4 June

John (Love) Jones b.1885

Pomp & Posterity – 1946–47

Pompey finished 12th in Division One with 41 points.

Pompey player born on 5 June

William (Bill) Joyce b.1877

— STAR & CRESCENT HERO – IKE CLARKE —

Born in Tipton, Staffordshire, on 9 January 1915 and the oldest member of Pompey's first League Championship-winning side, Isaac Clarke began playing in an amateur Wolverhampton league for Toll End Westley, and then signed as a professional for West Bromwich Albion, then a First Division club, in 1937. Ike was officially on their books for 10 years, but most of that career was lost through the Second World War. By the end of his time there, he had played 108 games and scored 39 goals.

As football began again in fits and starts after the war had ended, Ike eventually moved to Pompey in November 1947. West Bromwich were in the Second Division by then, and it is recorded that the Fratton Park faithful initially weren't very impressed that £7,000 had been spent on a striker already in his thirties from a lower division. Ike was to win them over and become one of the most popular players in the side.

Bob Jackson, the Pompey manager, had taken over a decent squad from Jack Tinn but he considered he needed Clarke for cover. He was a big brave centre-forward in the classic British tradition, but also had a good footballing brain and a good measure of skill.

Clarke came into the first team as a replacement for the injured Duggie Reid with a quarter of the 1948–49 season played and linked up the formidable forward line that Pompey boasted at that time. He was able to distribute the ball with accuracy and skill and held the line solidly. On his debut at Fratton Park, the day after he'd signed for Pompey, he scored against Aston Villa and went on to claim 14 goals in just 24 outings to help Pompey in their triumphant title campaign, taking the Championship for the first time in the club's history. Ten of those goals were hit in braces and one of them was hit home in the momentous game with Derby County in which a record 51,385 crowd squeezed into Fratton Park.

Ike's work as a probing and mobile striker was invaluable to Pompey. He scored some significant goals, but his 21st for Pompey was probably the most vital. Clarke had already played a part in the first goal at Burnden Park in April 1949 as Pompey moved closer to their most notable achievement to date when he headed in an ideal cross from Peter Harris to put Pompey 2–0 up. The game concluded with a 2–1 win for Pompey and, after the other results were checked, the boys from Fratton Park realised that they could not be caught and the League Championship was theirs.

Clarke's contribution to the Pompey cause in the following term was even greater. He had 37 outings and notched up 17 goals making him the club's top marksman. His jostling and pushing as an engine-like No. 9, along with Reid,

Harris (each scoring 16 goals) and Jack Froggatt (with 15 goals), helped Pompey to a total of 75 goals. Backed up by a miserly defence that was beaten just 38 times, the Blues successfully defended their title, lifting the Championship for the second time with the strength of their superior goal average.

Ike appeared intermittently in the 1950s and left Fratton Park at the age of 36; in his six years with Pompey, he'd clocked up 129 appearances (116 in the League) and 58 goals (49 in the League). Clarke also played five representative games for England ('B' Internationals were not awarded caps at that time) scoring 17 goals.

Ike took on the role of player-manager at Yeovil Town from 1953 to 1957. During that time, he led the club to victory in the Somerset Professional Cup, the Southern League Cup and the Southern League Championship Shield. Subsequently, he once more led the side to the finals of the Southern League and Somerset Professional Cups again, but lost each narrowly. His record at Yeovil reads: 218 played, 110 won, 49 drawn, 59 lost. As a player he made 103 appearances and scored 49 goals.

Clarke moved on to Sittingbourne FC with them and won the Kent League, Kent League Division One Cup, Kent Senior Cup and the Thames & Medway Combination League Championship. He took Sittingbourne into the Southern League Division One in 1959–60 and they missed out on promotion to the Premier Division on goal average. The same fate awaited them the following season.

Ike's final major post in football was as manager of Canterbury City, but he was Pools Manager at Chelmsford City from the late sixties.

Ike retired to Canterbury, living in the city until declining health saw him move to a Margate nursing home. Ike died aged 87 on 2 April 2002 after a short illness.

Pompey player born on 6 June

James Wallace Taylor (Jimmy) Guthrie b.1912

Pompey player born on 7 June

George James (Jimmy) Strong b.1916

Pompey player born on 8 June

Gerard (Gerry) Columba Bowler b.1919

Pomp & Posterity – 1947–48

Jack Tinn retired and Bob Jackson became manager of Pompey.

Pompey players born on 9 June
Christopher (Chris) James Clark b.1984; Vincent (Vince) Radcliffe b.1945; William Henry (Billy) Smith b.1906

— TRUE BLUE FACTS —

In May 1977 at York away, a Pompey fan climbed the scoreboard and released a banner which read 'I'll fix it'. He was referring to Pompey's caretaker manager Jimmy Dickinson – not Jimmy Saville! Pompey went on to win 3–1 that day.

In May 1987 before the final League game of the season at Fratton Park against Sheffield United, to celebrate the club's promotion to the old First Division, a Pompey fan scaled a floodlight pylon while the crowd chanted, 'Going up! Going up!' He was eventually talked down by the police.

Pompey are one of only seven clubs to win back-to-back titles.

Pompey player born on 10 June
Arthur Keeley b.1917

— STAR & CRESCENT HERO – ERNIE BUTLER —

The single ever-present player in the Pompey side that took the League Championships in 1949 and 1950, Ernie Butler let in only 80 League goals in those two glorious seasons, less than one a game. He maintained an unbelievable 17 clean sheets in the 1948/49 term.

Born at Box near Bath, Ernie was with Bath City before moving to Fratton Park in May 1938 for a fee of £100. A year later, when the Second World War broke out, Butler was off to the Far East to serve with the Royal Navy. Subsequently, he didn't make his Pompey debut until 1946. Ernie became first-choice keeper when the post-war programme started up again – in all, missing only a handful of matches from the end of the war up until August 1950.

Ernie made goalkeeping look easy and, in a side which contained the likes of Jack Froggatt, Duggie Reid and Len Phillips, it was felt that sometimes his efforts were overshadowed and he wasn't as appreciated by the fans as he might have been. Peter Harris, a good friend and former teammate of Butler's, said of Butler (with the authority of the club's record goal scorer), 'He was a good goalkeeper who dominated his area. He had the biggest hands in the business.'

Ernie lived in the North End area of Pompey and was never without his Championship medals, but, when he lost one, remarkably it was found in a street in North End and returned to him.

Alan Knight, another one-club Pompey keeper of the highest class, once said, 'I knew Ernie quite well and used to see him regularly when he lived in North End. Undoubtedly he was one of the greats.'

After 241 appearances for Pompey, Ernie retired in 1956 after breaking a hand in a reserve game. He had taken up greengrocery in the Milton area of Pompey, but later he managed the George and Dragon public house in the city's Kingston Road. He passed away in February 2002.

Pompey player born on 11 June

Sidney (Sid) Benjamin McClellan b.1925

Pompey player born on 12 June

John (Johnny) McIlwaine b.1904

Pomp & Posterity – 1948–49

The club had a double celebration in this season when they reached their Golden Jubilee and also won the First Division title. This success was reproduced the following year when in the final game of the season they beat Aston Villa 5–1 at Fratton Park to clinch the title ahead of Wolverhampton Wanderers.

— SEASON 1948–49 LEAGUE DIVISION 1 —

Date		Team	Result	Gate
21 Aug	A	Preston	D 2–2	32000
25 Aug	H	Everton	W 4–0	31000
28 Aug	H	Burnley	W 1–0	38000
01 Sept	A	Everton	W 5–0	40911
04 Sept	A	Stoke	W 1–0	30000
08 Sept	H	Middlesbrough	W 1–0	33000
11 Sept	H	Charlton	W 3–1	39000
15 Sept	A	Middlesbrough	D 1–1	35000
18 Sept	A	Man City	D 1–1	46372
25 Sept	H	Sheffield Utd	W 3–0	36000
02 Oct	H	Newcastle	W 1–0	44000
09 Oct	A	Aston Villa	D 1–1	55000
16 Oct	H	Sunderland	W 3–0	35000

23 Oct	A	Wolves	L	0–3	50000
30 Oct	H	Bolton	D	0–0	35000
06 Nov	A	Liverpool	L	1–3	43665
13 Nov	H	Blackpool	D	1–1	44000
20 Nov	A	Derby	L	0–1	34000
27 Nov	H	Arsenal	W	4–0	42500
4 Dec	A	Huddersfield	D	0–0	21785
11 Dec	H	Man Utd	D	2–2	30000
18 Dec	H	Preston	W	3–1	26000
25 Dec	A	Chelsea	W	2–1	42153
27 Dec	H	Chelsea	W	5–2	43000
01 Jan	A	Burnley	L	1–2	31305
15 Jan	H	Stoke	W	1–0	34000
22 Jan	A	Charlton	W	1–0	61475
05 Feb	H	Man City	W	3–1	35000
19 Feb	A	Sheffield Utd	L	1–3	46000
05 Mar	H	Aston Villa	W	3–0	34000
12 Mar	A	Sunderland	W	4–1	57229
19 Mar	H	Derby County	W	1–0	43000
02 Apr	H	Liverpool	W	3–2	34500
06 Apr	A	Newcastle	W	5–0	60611
09 Apr	A	Blackpool	L	1–0	29000
15 Apr	H	Birmingham	W	3–1	38000
16 Apr	H	Wolves	W	5–0	44000
18 Apr	A	Birmingham	L	3–0	30000
23 Apr	A	Bolton	W	2–1	28816
30 Apr	H	Huddersfield	W	2–0	36500
04 May	A	Arsenal	L	2–3	60000
07 May	A	Man Utd	L	2–3	39608

P42 W25 D8 L9 F84 A42 Pts 58

League Position 1st

Appearances: E Butler, P Rookes, H Ferrier, J Scoular, R Flewin, J Dickinson, P Harris, D Reid, J Froggatt, L Phillips, H Bowler, I Clark, J Yeuell, L Delapenha, C Parker, W Hindmarsh, W Thompson

Pompey players born on 13 June

F Henry Sparrow b.1889;

James (Jimmy) White b.1942

Pompey player born on 14 June

Hugh Henry Davey b.1897

Pompey player born on 15 June

Ivan Golac b.1950

Pompey player born on 16 June

Alexander (Alex) Govan b.1929

1948–49 League Division One

		P	W	D	L	F	A	W	D	L	F	A	Pts
1	Pompey	42	18	3	0	52	12	7	5	9	32	30	58
2	Manchester Utd	42	11	7	3	40	20	10	4	7	37	24	53
3	Derby County	42	17	2	2	48	22	5	7	9	26	33	53
4	Newcastle United	42	12	5	4	35	29	8	7	6	35	27	52
5	Arsenal	42	13	5	3	51	18	5	8	8	23	26	49
6	Wolverhampton W	42	13	5	3	48	19	4	7	10	31	47	46
7	Manchester City	42	10	8	3	28	21	5	7	9	19	30	45
8	Sunderland	42	8	10	3	27	19	5	7	9	22	39	43
9	Charlton Athletic	42	10	5	6	38	31	5	7	9	25	36	42
10	Aston Villa	42	10	6	5	40	36	6	4	11	20	40	42
11	Stoke City	42	14	3	4	43	24	2	6	13	23	44	41
12	Liverpool	42	5	10	6	25	18	8	4	9	28	25	40
13	Chelsea	42	10	6	5	43	27	2	8	11	26	41	38
14	Bolton W	42	10	4	7	43	32	4	6	11	16	36	38
15	Burnley	42	10	6	5	27	19	2	8	11	16	31	38
16	Blackpool	42	8	8	5	24	25	3	8	10	30	42	38
17	Birmingham City	42	9	7	5	19	10	2	8	11	17	28	37
18	Everton	42	12	5	4	33	25	1	6	14	8	38	37
19	Middlesbrough	42	10	6	5	37	23	1	6	14	9	34	34
20	Huddersfield Town	42	6	7	8	19	24	6	3	12	21	45	34
21	Preston NE	42	8	6	7	36	36	3	5	13	26	39	33
22	Sheffield Utd	42	8	9	4	32	25	3	2	16	25	53	33

Pompey players born on 17 June

John (Jack) Dixon Foxton b.1921;

Graeme James Hogg b.1964

— TO THE FRATTON FAITHFUL —

I saw them formed, I saw them in the mud and now they have won the League Championship.

Mr Sydney Leverett on the Board connected with the club since it was formed, on winning the first Championship, 1949

Pompey players born on 18 June
Russell (Russ) Perrett b.1973; Jamie Roy Vincent b.1975

Pompey player born on 19 June
Trevor Neal Hebberd b.1958

— TO THE FRATTON FAITHFUL —

Popular Chairman Mr Vernon Stokes had been a real inspiration to a grand side.

***The News* (after Pompey had won the League Championship in 1949)**

Pompey player born on 20 June
William (Bill 'Sunny' Jim) Kirby b.1882

— TRUE BLUE FACTS —

Bert Barlow is the only player to have gained an FA Cup winners' medal and a League Championship medal while with Pompey.

As punishment for being convicted of a public-order offence after some drunken behaviour in August 2000, the club fined both Rory Allen and Aaron Flahavan two weeks' wages – £12,000 – which Stevie Claridge put to good use financing a day out at Cheltenham races!

Pompey player born on 21 June
Thomas (Tommy) Bowman b.1972

Pomp & Posterity – 1949–50

Pompey retained the Championship; however, this achievement was accomplished by the narrowest of margins. Pompey and Wolves finished with 53 points, but Portsmouth's goal average of 1.95 bettered Wolves' 1.55.

Pompey player born on 22 June
Herbert James (Bert) Leavey b.1886

Pompey player born on 23 June
Hayden Foxe b.1977

— SEASON 1949–50 LEAGUE DIVISION 1 —

Date		Team	Result	Gate
20 Aug	A	Newcastle	W 3–1	45000
24 Aug	H	Man City	D 1–1	44297
27 Aug	H	Blackpool	L 2–3	44815
31 Aug	A	Man City	L 0–1	32631
03 Sept	A	Middlesbrough	W 5–1	45000
05 Sept	A	Aston Villa	L 0–1	48000
10 Sept	H	Everton	W 7–0	36054
17 Sept	A	Huddersfield	W 1–0	26222
24 Sept	H	Bolton	D 1–1	35765
01 Oct	H	Wolves	D 1–1	50248
08 Oct	A	Birmingham	W 3–0	38000
15 Oct	H	Derby	W 3–1	37340
22 Oct	A	WBA	L 0–3	40000
29 Oct	H	Man Utd	D 0–0	41098
05 Nov	A	Chelsea	W 4–1	31650
12 Nov	H	Stoke	D 0–0	33257
19 Nov	A	Burnley	L 1–2	28500
26 Nov	H	Sunderland	D 2–2	36707
03 Dec	A	Liverpool	D 2–2	44851
10 Dec	H	Arsenal	W 2–1	39537
17 Dec	H	Newcastle	W 1–0	30455
24 Dec	A	Blackpool	L 2–1	27000
26 Dec	A	Charlton	W 2–1	38000
27 Dec	H	Charlton	W 1–0	43650
31 Dec	H	Middlesbrough	D 1–1	33364
14 Jan	A	Everton	W 2–1	50421
21 Jan	H	Huddersfield	W 4–0	29746
04 Feb	A	Bolton	L 2–1	29284
18 Feb	A	Wolves	L 0–1	40000
25 Feb	H	Birmingham	W 2–0	28429

08 Mar	A	Derby	L	2–1	17000
11 Mar	H	Burnley	W	2–1	26728
18 Mar	A	Sunderland	D	2–2	44591
25 Mar	H	Chelsea	W	2–0	28574
01 Apr	A	Stoke	W	1–0	27000
07 Apr	H	Fulham	W	3–0	39342
08 Apr	H	WBA	L	0–1	33903
10 Apr	A	Fulham	W	1–0	43716
15 Apr	A	Man Utd	W	2–1	44908
22 Apr	H	Liverpool	W	2–0	47507
03 May	A	Arsenal	L	2–0	65000
06 May	H	Aston Villa	W	5–1	42295

P42 W22 D9 L11 F74 A38 Pts 53
League Position 1st

Appearances: E Butler, J Yeuell, H Ferrier, J Scoular, R Flewin, J Dickinson, P Harris, D Reid, I Clarke, Len Phillips, J Froggatt, W Hindmarsh, L Delapenha, W Thompson, R Pickett, J Dawson, H Barlow, C Parker, W Spence, J Stephen, J Elder, D Ekner, P Rookes, P Higham, R Bennett

Pompey player born on 24 June
Colin John Sullivan b.1951

Pompey player born on 25 June
Richard Daniel Hughes b.1979

— TO THE FRATTON FAITHFUL —

As he addressed the crowd who had started to sing Happy Birthday, he announced that it was his birthday and spoke of Portsmouth's victory as a wonderful present.

The Lord Mayor of Portsmouth (Alderman John Privett at the Victory Parade celebrating Pompey's League Championship Monday, 8 May 1950)

Pompey player born on 26 June
William (Billy) Harker b.1911

Pompey player born on 27 June
Leonard Daniel (Len) McCarthy b.1905

1949–50 League Division One

		P	W	D	L	F	A	W	D	L	F	A	Pts
1	Pompey	42	12	7	2	44	15	10	2	9	30	23	53
2	Wolverhampton W	42	11	8	2	47	21	9	5	7	29	28	53
3	Sunderland	42	14	6	1	50	23	7	4	10	33	39	52
4	Manchester Utd	42	11	5	5	42	20	7	9	5	27	24	50
5	Newcastle	42	14	4	3	49	23	5	8	8	28	32	50
6	Arsenal	42	12	4	5	48	24	7	7	7	31	31	49
7	Blackpool	42	10	8	3	29	14	7	7	7	17	21	49
8	Liverpool	42	10	7	4	37	23	7	7	7	27	31	48
9	Middlesbrough	42	14	2	5	37	18	6	5	10	22	30	47
10	Burnley	42	9	7	5	23	17	7	6	8	17	23	45
11	Derby County	42	11	5	5	46	26	6	5	10	23	35	44
12	Aston Villa	42	10	7	4	31	19	5	5	11	30	42	42
13	Chelsea	42	7	7	7	31	30	5	9	7	27	35	40
14	West Brom	42	9	7	5	28	16	5	5	11	19	37	40
15	Huddersfield	42	11	4	6	34	22	3	5	13	18	51	37
16	Bolton W	42	10	5	6	34	22	0	9	12	11	37	34
17	Fulham	42	8	6	7	24	19	2	8	11	17	35	34
18	Everton	42	6	8	7	24	20	4	6	11	18	46	34
19	Stoke City	42	10	4	7	27	28	1	8	12	18	47	34
20	Charlton Athletic	42	7	5	9	33	35	6	1	14	20	30	32
21	Manchester City	42	7	8	6	27	24	1	5	15	9	44	29
22	Birmingham	42	6	8	7	19	24	1	6	14	12	43	28

Pompey player born on 28 June

Alfred G Gittens b.1886

Pompey players born on 29 June

Colin Arthur Garwood b.1949; Andrew (Andy) James O'Brien b.1979

Pomp & Posterity – 3 May 1950

Pompey went into the game needing victory to ensure their 100 per cent record against London clubs for the season. Unfortunately, it was not to be as the Blues crashed 2–0 in front of 20,000 Pompey fans who made the trip to Highbury.

Pompey player born on 30 June

William John (Billy) Moffatt b.1897

Pompey player born on 1 July
Arthur Edward Elsdon b.1882

— TRUE BLUE FACTS —

Pompey player Reg Pickett was born in Bareilly, India.

It was rumoured that the Pompey builders who were involved in building the new S***hampton ground had applied a chemical solution to the brickwork so that, when it rained, 'Portsmouth FC' would be seen on the side of the ground.

There are also rumours of Pompey shirts buried underneath the centre circle, as well as vegetable seed, from which, when grown, the word Pompey will appear!

Pompey player born on 2 July
John W (Jack) Surtees b.1911

Pompey players born on 3 July
Sveom Are Andreassen b.1968; Lee Michael Bradbury b.1975; Graham Paul Roberts b.1959

POMPEY PUB
The Rutland Arms
Francis Avenue, Southsea

— POMPEY XIs – PFC v SFC —

*Here are 11 of Pompey's wins against S***hampton:*

Date	Result
24-04-2005	Pompey 4 – S***hampton 1
21-03-2004	Pompey 1 – S***hampton 0
03-01-1988	S***hampton 0 – Pompey 2
08-02-1964	Pompey 3 – S***hampton 2
28-09-1963	Pompey 2 – S***hampton 0
07-05-1934	Pompey 4 – S***hampton 1
03-05-1933	Pompey 5 – S***hampton 0
11-05-1932	Pompey 5 – S***hampton 1
04-05-1931	Pompey 4 – S***hampton 0
07-05-1930	Pompey 2 – S***hampton 0
07-05-1928	Pompey 6 – S***hampton 1

Pompey players born on 4 July

John Ashworth b.1937;

Terence (Terry) William Brisley b.1950;

Lionel Arthur Louch b.1888

Pompey player born on 5 July

John Law (Johnny) McNeil b.1906

Pompey players born on 6 July

John W (Joe) Davison b.1897; Alan James Rogers b.1954

Pompey player born on 7 July

Michael Henry (Harry) Proctor b.1912

— TRUE BLUE FACTS —

In 1951, Pompey went on an end-of-season tour of Brazil, losing three games and drawing three.

Pompey were threatened with having points deducted if their fans, who invaded the pitch during the Crystal Palace game (2000/2001 season), played up again!

However, on 22 September in the following season, Pompey fans ran riot when they visited Coventry at Highfield Road. Pompey's captain Scott Hiley said, 'I can't understand why so-called fans would want to behave like this. We don't want them anywhere near this club.'

Pompey were lucky to escape without a point's deduction.

Pompey players born on 8 July

William (Billy) Bagley b.1909;

Thomas (Tommy) Frederick Youlden b.1949

Pompey player born on 9 July

Stanley (Stan) James William Earl b.1929

Pomp & Posterity – 1952–55

Under manager Bob Jackson, Pompey managed fourth place in the 1951/52 season. Jackson left and was replaced by Eddie Lever whose most notable success was a third-place finish in the 1954/55 season.

(Chelsea won with Wolves finishing as runners-up.)

Pompey player born on 10 July
William (Billy) Wilson b.1946

Pompey player born on 11 July
Arthur George Marshall b.1880

— TRUE BLUE FACTS —

The original floodlights at Fratton Park were installed in 1953.

Pompey's Alessandro Zamperini wore the No. 13 shirt, not a first choice for any player, especially Italians, but in recognition of his idol Alessandro Nesta.

Pompey player born on 12 July
Joseph (Joe) Daniel Laidlaw b.1950

Pompey player born on 13 July
Raymond (Ray) Crawford b.1936

Pompey players born on 14 July
Andrew (Andy) Terence Awford b.1972;
Wyndham William Pretoria (Willie) Haines b.1900;
Richard (Dick) John Pearson b.1931

Players who have played League football for Pompey and then gone on to manage the club

Ron Tindall
Jimmy Dickinson
Bobby Campbell
Tony Barton (caretaker)
Steve Claridge (caretaker)
Bill Thompson (caretaker

Pompey players born on 15 July
Carl Brian Griffiths b.1971; John (Jackie) Craig Robertson b.1928

Pompey player born on 16 July
Robert G (Bobby) Marshall b.1876

Pompey player born on 17 July
Keith Blackburn b.1940

— POMPEY SPONSORS IN THE LAST 20 YEARS —

1987–88	South Coast Fiat
1988–89	No sponsor
1989–95	Goodman's
1995–97	*The News*
1997–99	KJC
1999–2000	The 'Pompey Centre'
2000–2002	Bishops Printers
2002–2005	TY
2005–to date	OKI Printing Solutions

Pompey players born on 18 July

Henry Michael (Mike) Barnard b.1933; Sasa Ilic b.1972

Pompey player born on 19 July

Henry (Harry) Penk b.1934

Pompey players born on 20 July

Thomas (Tommy) Anton Christensen b.1961; Rowan Lee Mills b.1970; Nigel Francis Quashie b.1978

Pomp & Posterity – 1956–57

Pompey finished fourth from bottom in Division One, their lowest position since 1938.

— STAR & CRESCENT HERO – DAVID KEMP —

Despite only playing for Pompey for two incomplete seasons (1976–77 and 1977–78), Kemp was the club's top goal scorer during that time.

He signed for Pompey in November 1976 from Crystal Palace in a deal secured by then manager Ian St John. Pompey were in desperate need of a goal scorer after finding themselves in the lower part of Division Three. Kemp's rate of scoring saw off the threat of relegation, for that season at least, before he left the club in early 1978 for Carlisle United. He returned to Pompey in December 1999 in a coaching role but left when manager Tony Pulis was sacked.

During his spell at Pompey, Kemp's goal-scoring record was an impressive 32 in 64 league appearances.

Pompey player born on 21 July
Anthony James Pulis b.1984

Pompey players born on 22 July
Herbert (Bert) Barlow b.1916;
Raymond (Ray) Michael Charles Hiron b.1943;
John (Jack) Friar b.1911

Pompey player born on 23 July
Murdoch McKenzie b.1900

POMPEY PUB
The Milton Arms
Milton Road, Milton

Pompey player born on 24 July
(Preki) Predrag Radosavljevic b.1963

Pomp & Posterity – 1957–58
Pompey avoided relegation on goal difference.

Pompey player born on 25 July
Sidney (Sid) Binks b.1889

— TRUE BLUE FACT —

Pompey conceded 112 goals in the 1958/9 season, the most the club has ever conceded.

— POMPEY'S FIRST POST-WAR LEAGUE MATCH —

Pompey 3 – Blackburn 1
31 August 1946
Attendance: 30,962

— POMPEY RESERVE GAME HIGHEST ATTENDANCE —

Pompey 5 – Charlton 1
1 March 1952
Attendance: 30,289

1958–59 League Division One													
		P	**W**	**D**	**L**	**F**	**A**	**W**	**D**	**L**	**F**	**A**	**Pts**
1	Wolverhampton W	42	15	3	3	68	19	13	2	6	42	30	61
2	Manchester Utd	42	14	4	3	58	27	10	3	8	45	39	55
3	Arsenal	42	14	3	4	53	29	7	5	9	35	39	50
4	Bolton W	42	14	3	4	56	30	6	7	8	23	36	50
5	West Brom	42	8	7	6	41	33	10	6	5	47	35	49
6	West Ham Utd	42	15	3	3	59	29	6	3	12	26	41	48
7	Burnley	42	11	4	6	41	29	8	6	7	40	41	48
8	Blackpool	42	12	7	2	39	13	6	4	11	27	36	47
9	Birmingham	42	14	1	6	54	35	6	5	10	30	33	46
10	Blackburn Rovers	42	12	3	6	48	28	5	7	9	28	42	44
11	Newcastle Utd	42	11	3	7	40	29	6	4	11	40	51	41
12	Preston NE	42	9	3	9	40	39	8	4	9	30	38	41
13	Nottingham Forest	42	9	4	8	37	32	8	2	11	34	42	40
14	Chelsea	42	13	2	6	52	37	5	2	14	25	61	40
15	Leeds Utd	42	8	7	6	28	27	7	2	12	29	47	39
16	Everton	42	11	3	7	39	38	6	1	14	32	49	38
17	Luton Town	42	11	6	4	50	26	1	7	13	18	45	37
18	Tottenham	42	10	3	8	56	42	3	7	11	29	53	36
19	Leicester City	42	7	6	8	34	36	4	4	13	33	62	32
20	Manchester City	42	8	7	6	40	32	3	2	16	24	63	31
21	Aston Villa	42	8	5	8	31	33	3	3	15	27	54	30
22	**Pompey**	**42**	**5**	**4**	**12**	**38**	**47**	**1**	**5**	**15**	**26**	**65**	**21**

Pompey player born on 26 July

Mladen Rudonja b.1971

Pompey player born on 27 July

Harry J Frampton b.1896

Pomp & Posterity – 1958–59

Pompey relegated after 32 years in the top flight.

After a couple of mediocre seasons, Lever was replaced by Freddie Cox. Cox's reign saw Pompey win only six games of the 42, finishing bottom of the League and relegated on 21 points.

Pompey player born on 28 July
Frederick T (Fred) Thompson b.1875

Pompey player born on 29 July
James Crossley b.1922

Pompey players born on 30 July
Anthony (Tony) Macken b.1950; Neil John Webb b.1963

Pompey player born on 31 July
Brian Alfred Turner b.1949

— TRUE BLUE FACT —

Ex-Pompey forward 'Lindy' Delapenha went on to represent Jamaica at golf.

Pompey players born on 1 August
Terence (Terry) John Bell b.1944;
James (Jimmy) Robert Glass b.1973;
David Benjamin James b.1970; Nwankwo Kanu b.1976

Pompey player born on 2 August
Frederick Ernest John (Fred) Chandler b.1912

— PLAYERS WITH TWO SPELLS OF LEAGUE FOOTBALL WITH POMPEY —

Johnny Gordon
Pat Neil
Brian Lewis
Bobby Kellard
Eoin Hand
Chris Kamara
Paul Wood
Paul Walsh
Guy Whittingham
Lee Bradbury

Pompey players born on 3 August
Ronald (Ron) Howells b.1935; Michael (Micky) James Lill b.1936

Pompey player born on 4 August
William (Billy) Lee b.1878

Pompey player born on 5 August
Harold (Harry) Moore b. 1896

Pompey player born on 6 August
Ronald (Ron) William Tilsed b.1952

— PLAYER OF THE SEASON —

1971 – David Munks
1972 – Richard Reynolds
1973 – Not Awarded
1974 – Paul Went
1975 – Mick Mellows
1976 – Norman Piper
1977 – Not Awarded
1978 – Not Awarded
1979 – Peter Mellor
1980 – Joe Laidlaw
1981 – Keith Vinney
1982 – Alan Knight
1983 – Alan Biley
1984 – Mark Hateley
1985 – Neil Webb
1986 – Noel Blake
1987 – Noel Blake
1988 – Barry Horne
1989 – Mick Quinn
1990 – Guy Whittingham
1991 – Martin Kuhl
1992 – Darren Anderton
1993 – Paul Walsh
1994 – Kit Symons
1995 – Alan Knight
1996 – Alan Knight
1997 – Lee Bradbury
1998 – Andy Awford
1999 – Steve Claridge
2000 – Steve Claridge
2001 – Scott Hiley
2002 – Lewis Buxton
2003 – Svetoslav Todorov
2004 – Linvoy Primus
2005 – Dejan Stefanovic
2006 – Gary O'Neil

— POMPEY PLAYER OF THE SEASON XI —

Of those players awarded 'player of the season' since the 1970s, here's how our best possible XI would line up:

Alan Knight

David Munks — Paul Went — Arjan De Zeeuw — Noel Blake

Darren Anderton — Mark Kuhl — Neil Webb — Norman Piper

Alan Biley — Mark Hateley

Subs

Peter Mellor, Mick Mellows, Mick Quinn, Guy Whittingham, Paul Walsh

Pompey players born on 7 August
Richard Charles (Charlie) Brittan b.1887;
Michael (Micky) James Reid b.1927

— TRUE BLUE SONG —

Knees up Mother Brown,
Knees up Mother Brown
Under the table you must go
E I E I E I O
If I catch you bending
I'll saw your legs right off
So knees up, knees up, don't get the breeze up
Knees up Mother Brown
Oh my what a rotten song,
What a rotten song,
What a rotten song,
Oh my what a rotten song
And what a rotten singer tooooooooooooooh.

Pompey player born on 8 August
James Phillips (Jimmy) Knox b.1910

Pompey player born on 9 August
George Charles Hunter b.1896

— TRUE BLUE FACT —

Ray Hiron signed professionally for Pompey during his lunch break from the Naval Dockyard in Portsmouth.

Pompey players born on 10 August
William Frederick Albury b.1933;
Andrew (Andy) Charles Cook b.1969;
William (Bill) Gordon Thompson b.1921

Pompey players born on 11 August
Thomas (Tommy) Graham Brown b.1924;
Robert Nelson (Bob) White b.1902

1960–61 League Division Two		P	W	D	L	F	A	W	D	L	F	A	Pts
1	Ipswich Town	42	15	3	3	55	24	11	4	6	45	31	59
2	Sheffield Utd	42	16	2	3	49	22	10	4	7	32	29	58
3	Liverpool	42	14	5	2	49	21	7	5	9	38	37	52
4	Norwich City	42	15	3	3	46	20	5	6	10	24	33	49
5	Middlesbrough	42	13	6	2	44	20	5	6	10	39	54	48
6	Sunderland	42	12	5	4	47	24	5	8	8	28	36	47
7	Swansea City	42	14	4	3	49	26	4	7	10	28	47	47
8	S***hampton	42	12	4	5	57	35	6	4	11	27	46	44
9	Scunthorpe	42	9	8	4	39	25	5	7	9	30	39	43
10	Charlton Athletic	42	12	3	6	60	42	4	8	9	37	49	43
11	Plymouth Argyle	42	13	4	4	52	32	4	4	13	29	50	42
12	Derby County	42	9	6	6	46	35	6	4	11	34	45	40
13	Luton Town	42	13	5	3	48	27	2	4	15	23	52	39
14	Leeds Utd	42	7	7	7	41	38	7	3	11	34	45	38
15	Rotherham	42	9	7	5	37	24	3	6	12	28	40	37
16	Brighton HA	42	9	6	6	33	26	5	3	13	28	49	37
17	Bristol Rovers	42	13	4	4	52	35	2	3	16	21	57	37
18	Stoke City	42	9	6	6	39	26	3	6	12	12	33	36
19	Leyton Orient	42	10	5	6	31	29	4	3	14	24	49	36
20	Huddersfield Town	42	7	5	9	33	33	6	4	11	29	38	35
21	**Pompey**	**42**	**10**	**6**	**5**	**38**	**27**	**1**	**5**	**15**	**26**	**64**	**33**
22	Lincoln City	42	5	4	12	30	43	3	4	14	18	52	24

Pomp & Posterity – 1960–61

The 1960s did not get off to a good start when Pompey were relegated to the Third Division in 1961.

February 1961 also saw the dismissal of Freddie Cox who was replaced by George Smith in April.

Pompey player born on 12 August

Benjamin (Ben) Lewis b.1898

Pompey players born on 13 August

Niko Kranjcar b.1984;

John (Jock) McHugh b.1909;

Benjani Mwaruwari b.1978

Above: The Fratton End Faithful.

Below: Pompey 'til we die.

Inside and outside view of Fratton Park.

Above: The 1983 Division 3 Championship winners.

Below: Pompey favourites Paul Walsh and Guy Whittingham.

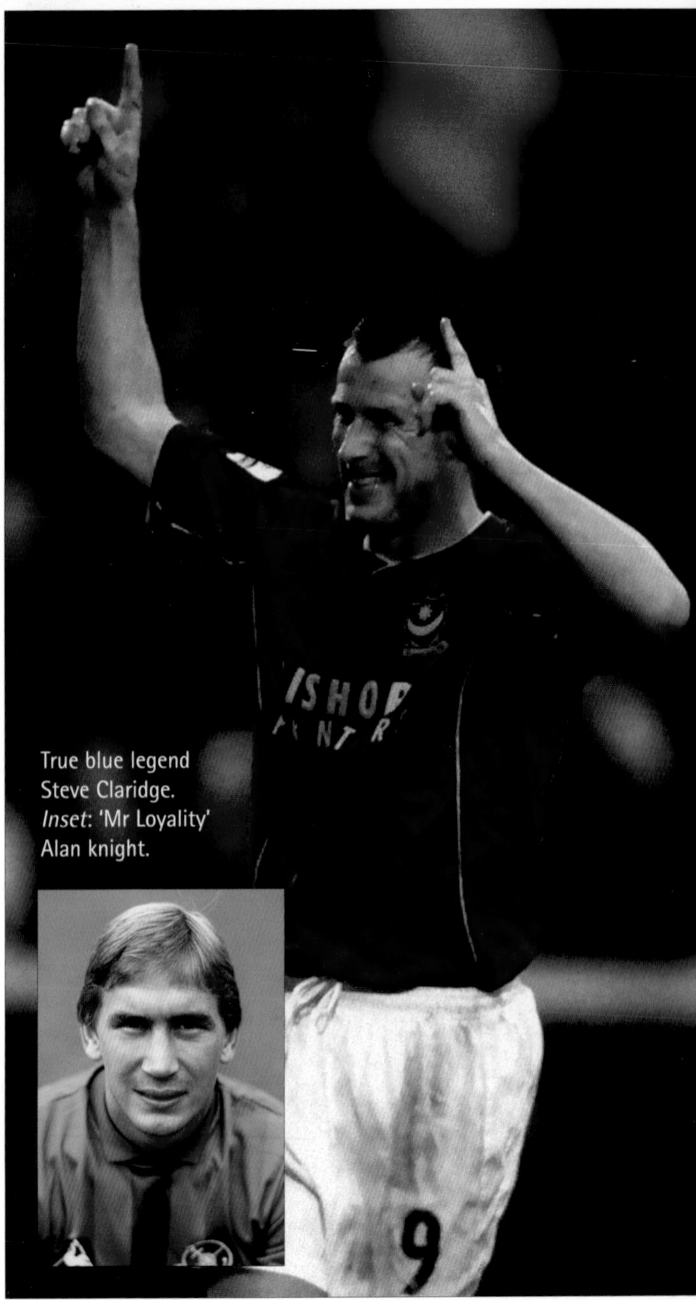

True blue legend Steve Claridge. *Inset*: 'Mr Loyality' Alan knight.

Portsmouth F.C.
1898-1910
1921-32
1937-56
1958-66
1966-71
1971-72
1973-74
1976-77
1979-80
1980-82
1980-82 (a)
1982-83
1982-83 (a)
1983-85
1983-85 (a)
1983-85 (3)
1985-87
1985-87 (a)
1985-87 (3)
1987-89
1987-89 (a)
1989-91
1989-91 (a)
1991-93
1991-93 (a)
1993-95
1993-95 (a)
1994-96 (3)
1995-97
1995-97 (a)
1996-97 (3)
1997-99
1997-99 (a)
1998-99 (3)
1999-00
1999-00 (a)
2000-02
2000-02 (a)
2000-02
2002-03
2002-03 (a)
2002-04 (3)
2003-05
2003-05 (a)
2004-05 (3)
2005-06
2005-06 (a)
2005-06 (3)
2006-07
2006-07 (a)
©www.kitclassics.co.uk
Portsmouth

Pompey kit classics 1898–2007

'Land spotting' John PFC Westwood style

Top: Merse, Yak and Matty = quality in a Pompey shirt.

Left: Harry and Jim.

Below: Nationwide Division 1 Champions 2003.

Play up Pompey, we love y

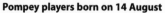

Pompey players born on 14 August
Martin James Allen b.1965;
Ralph Robert Arthur Hunt b.1933

Pompey players born on 15 August
Yoshikatsu Kwaguchi b.1975;
Alessandro Zamperini b.1982

Pomp & Posterity – 1961–62

Manager George Smith led Pompey as they bounced back as Division Three champions.

Pompey player born on 16 August
John Richard (Jack) Lewis b.1881

Pompey player born on 17 August
Peter William Price b.1949

Pompey players born on 18 August
Mark James Burchill b.1980;
John Paul Durnin b.1965;
Keith Andrew James b.1961

— TRUE BLUE FACT —

Fratton Park is the only League ground in England built on a natural island.

Pompey player born on 19 August
Arthur George Baxter b.1910

Pompey players born on 20 August
Brett Ashley Mark Angell b.1968;
Philip (Phil) Eric Figgins b.1955;
Steven (Steve) Brian Stone b.1971

— SEASON 1961–62 LEAGUE DIVISION 3 —

Date		Team	Result	Gate
19 Aug	A	Swindon	W 3–1	16153
23 Aug	H	Southend	W 1–0	18893
26 Aug	H	Halifax	D 1–1	15322
28 Aug	A	Southend	D 2–2	12827
02 Sept	A	QPR	W 1–0	12856
06 Sept	H	Lincoln City	D 0–0	13271
09 Sept	H	Barnsley	W 3–2	16014
16 Sept	H	Newport	D 2–2	14006
20 Sept	A	Torquay	W 2–0	6119
23 Sept	A	C Palace	W 2–1	24586
27 Sept	H	Torquay	W 2–0	14546
30 Sept	H	Bournemouth	D 1–1	25672
07 Oct	A	Notts Co	L 1–2	9889
11 Oct	H	Hull City	W 2–1	14107
14 Oct	H	Shrewsbury	W 3–1	16683
21 Oct	A	Brentford	L 2–3	9600
28 Oct	H	Reading	W 2–0	18811
11 Nov	H	Bradford PA	W 4–2	11546
18 Nov	A	Grimsby	L 0–1	6889
02 Dec	A	Peterborough	W 1–0	14289
09 Dec	H	Port Vale	W 1–0	11925
16 Dec	H	Swindon	D 2–2	13990
23 Dec	A	Halifax	W 1–0	4122
26 Dec	H	Northampton	W 4–1	17396
06 Jan	A	Hull City	W 1–0	6454
13 Jan	H	QPR	W 4–1	8229
20 Jan	A	Barnsley	D 2–2	5992
27 Jan	H	Coventry	W 3–2	13405
05 Feb	A	Newport Co	W 5–0	7000
10 Feb	H	C Palace	W 2–1	22541
17 Feb	A	Bournemouth	L 0–2	22942
24 Feb	H	Notts Co	D 0–0	14438
03 Mar	A	Shrewsbury	W 1–0	5745
06 Mar	A	Bristol City	W 4–0	21802
10 Mar	H	Brentford	W 4–0	15256
16 Mar	A	Reading	W 3–0	22969

20 Mar	A	Northampton	D 2–2	13622
24 Mar	H	Bristol City	W 5–0	20584
31 Mar	A	Bradford PA	L 1–2	10154
07 Apr	H	Grimsby	L 0–2	19285
14 Apr	A	Coventry	L 0–2	9711
20 Apr	A	Watford	D 0–0	12657
21 Apr	H	Peterborough	L 0–3	21167
23 Apr	H	Watford	W 2–1	18139
28 Apr	A	Port Vale	W 3–2	6071
02 May	A	Lincoln C	D 2–2	3316

P46 W27 D11 L8 F87 A47 Pts 65
League Position 1st (Promoted as Champions)

Appearances: R Beattie, C Rutter, A Wilson, R Smith, J Dickinson, A Priscott, R Saunders, H Middleton, R Cutler, P Shearing, P Gunter, A Brown, B Snowdon, H Harris, J Campbell, J Gordon, J White, K Blackburn, S Chapman, R Campbell, A Barton, D Dodson

Pompey players born on 21 August
Thomas (Billy) William Bushby b.1914;
James (Jimmy) Martin b.1898;
Alfred (Alfie) George Edward Noakes b.1933;
Edward Riddle (Ted) Robson b.1890; Paul Simon Ritchie b.1975;
Hamilton Thorp b.1973

Pomp & Posterity – 1963–64
Centre-forward Ron Saunders scored 33 goals.

Pompey players born on 22 August
Roberto (Robbie) Manuel Enes b.1975;
John (Jack) Mansell b.1927

Pompey players born on 23 August
Graham Roy Horn b.1954;
Glen McLeod Johnson b.1984;
James (Jimmy) Findlay Stephen b.1922;
Michael (Mike) Joseph Patrick Travers b.1942;
William (Bill) Thomas Williams b.1942

1961–62 League Division Three												
	P	W	D	L	F	A	W	D	L	F	A	Pts
1 Pompey	**46**	**15**	**6**	**2**	**48**	**23**	**12**	**5**	**6**	**39**	**24**	**65**
2 Grimsby Town	46	18	3	2	49	18	10	3	10	31	38	62
3 Bournemouth	46	14	8	1	42	18	7	9	7	27	27	59
4 QPR	46	15	3	5	65	31	9	8	6	46	42	59
5 Peterborough	46	16	0	7	60	38	10	6	7	47	44	58
6 Bristol City	46	15	3	5	56	27	8	5	10	38	45	54
7 Reading	46	14	5	4	46	24	8	4	11	31	42	53
8 Northampton	46	12	6	5	52	24	8	5	10	33	33	51
9 Swindon Town	46	11	8	4	48	26	6	7	10	30	45	49
10 Hull City	46	15	2	6	43	20	5	6	12	24	34	48
11 Bradford PA	46	13	5	5	47	27	7	2	14	33	51	47
12 Port Vale	46	12	4	7	41	23	5	7	11	24	35	45
13 Notts County	46	14	5	4	44	23	3	4	16	23	51	43
14 Coventry City	46	11	6	6	38	26	5	5	13	26	45	43
15 Crystal Palace	46	8	8	7	50	41	6	6	11	33	39	42
16 Southend Utd	46	10	7	6	31	26	3	9	11	26	43	42
17 Watford	46	10	9	4	37	26	4	4	15	26	48	41
18 Halifax Town	46	9	5	9	34	35	6	5	12	28	49	40
19 Shrewsbury	46	8	7	8	46	37	5	5	13	27	47	38
20 Barnsley	46	9	6	8	45	41	4	6	13	26	54	38
21 Torquay Utd	46	9	4	10	48	44	6	2	15	28	56	36
22 Lincoln City	46	4	10	9	31	43	5	7	11	26	44	35
23 Brentford	46	11	3	9	34	29	2	5	16	19	64	34
24 Newport County	46	6	5	12	29	38	1	3	19	17	64	22

— STAR & CRESCENT HERO – ALAN BILEY —

Alan Biley was a very popular player in the early 1980s and was very much part of the team which saw Pompey rise from the Fourth/Third Division side of the late 1970s to the upper reaches of the Second Division in the mid-1980s. He was signed for Pompey in the summer of 1982 from Everton by then manager Bobby Campbell.

Biley was the final piece in Campbell's jigsaw for the upcoming season; his other signings that summer included Neil Webb. Upon completing the signing of Biley, Campbell confidently predicted that Pompey would finish top of the League. His confidence was well founded, with Pompey winning the Third Division in the 1982–83 season. Biley finished top scorer with 23 goals.

By the time the 1983–84 season had started, Mark Hateley had been signed and Biley formed a successful partnership with him, netting 43 goals between the two of them over the season.

Biley was certainly a fans' favourite and had many memorable games for the club, none more so than against Oxford United at Fratton Park in December 1984. Pompey were trailing 0–1 until the dying minutes when a fan dressed as Santa invaded the pitch. This brought some additional injury time during which Biley managed to score two goals, winning the match for Pompey.

Alan Ball made the decision to sell Biley to Brighton for £50,000 at the end of the 1984–85 season – a decision that was deeply unpopular with the fans.

Pompey players born on 24 August
Michael Lauriston Thomas b.1967;
Kenneth (Kenny) Todd b.1957

Pomp & Posterity – 1964–65

Pompey said goodbye to 'Gentleman Jim' Jimmy Dickinson as he neared his 40th birthday. Twenty thousand fans turned up to see the Pompey legend play his final game for the club. This was a relegation battle which saw Pompey avoid the drop with a late goal securing the one point required for Second Division survival. Jimmy is still Pompey's longest-serving player.

Pompey player born on 25 August
Richard Matiland b.1900

Pompey player born on 26 August
Peter Fraser Shearing b.1938

— TRUE BLUE FACT —

In 1965, Pompey scrapped their reserve and youth teams; one of the released players was future England captain Mick Mills.

Pompey players born on 27 August
Ian Philip Drummond b.1923; Norman Field b.1927

Pompey player born on 28 August
Leonard Aubrey Mandy b.1905

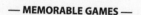

— MEMORABLE GAMES —

Northampton Town v Pompey (County Ground)
24 April 1965
Result: 1–1
Pompey goal scorer: Wilson

Although Pompey had played one season in Division Three in the 1961–62 season, the gradual decline since the Championship-winning years continued as they found themselves going into this match needing a point to avoid relegation.

Further significance was added to this game by the fact that it was to be the last match of Jimmy Dickinson's playing career.

The odds were stacked against Pompey as Northampton had had a good season and went into the game already promoted to Division One. Things looked grim when, late in the second half, Pompey striker Johnny Gordon scored an own goal.

However, with less than 10 minutes to go, a Pompey corner resulted in a goal from full-back Alex Wilson. Survival was assured for another season and Jimmy Dickinson left the pitch for the last time with the Chimes ringing out.

Pompey player born on 29 August
John (Jack) Price b.1918

Pompey player born on 30 August
Svetoslav Todorov b.1978

Pomp & Posterity – 1965–66

The Pompey squad was only 16-strong. The reserve and youth teams were axed due to lack of money, and George Smith's opinion on local talent was clear enough when he said, 'There is nothing around Pompey except fish'.

Pompey player born on 31 August
George Henry Russell b.1902

Pompey player born on 1 September
Robert McGregor b.1890

— STAR & CRESCENT HERO – JIMMY DICKINSON —

Born in Alton in 1925, Jimmy Dickinson holds a unique place in the history of Portsmouth Football Club. 'Gentleman Jim' was one of the great figures in football throughout the game's golden age following the Second World War, a time when supporters came to football in their millions.

Jimmy came to Fratton Park as a trainee from Alton Youth Club, having been recommended by his maths and PE teacher Eddie Lever, who would go on to manage his former pupil at Fratton Park.

Following three years' national service in the Royal Navy, Jimmy made his League debut on 31 August 1946 at Fratton Park against Blackburn Rovers.

Swiftly settling into the team, Dickinson made the No. 6 shirt his own and assisted Pompey to consecutive League Championships. His solid, reliable and not inconspicuous performances brought him international recognition and he eventually made a total of 48 appearances for England, which made him Pompey's most capped player of all time.

Jim appeared in 764 League games for Pompey, a record for one player at a single club, which was not broken until 1980 when Swindon's John Trollope hit 770. In all, he netted nine times for the Blues.

Dickinson was a rock for Pompey for nearly two decades and was awarded the MBE in 1964.

Jimmy was a gentleman on and off the pitch. In 812 games for England and Pompey, he was never booked or sent off. His hard-working and definite approach on either wing-half or at left-half was renowned in what was probably the best half-back line (alongside Jack Froggatt and Jimmy Scoular) England has known.

When Jim retired from playing, he continued to serve Pompey as public relations officer and then secretary, before unwillingly accepting the job as manager in May 1977. He was able to temporarily steer the club clear of relegation from the Third Division, but the next season Pompey fell into the basement of English football.

The strain of managing the club in the Fourth Division hit Jim's health. He suffered three heart attacks and passed away on 9 November 1982 aged just 57. The famous 'Pompey Chimes' echoed evocatively around St Mary's Church in Fratton at a packed memorial service for the greatly loved hero.

In 1998 Jim was included on the list of 100 Legends produced to celebrate the centenary of the Football League.

Today his image can be seen in the seating of the Fratton End stand.

Pompey player born on 2 September
Michael (Micky) Patrick Ross b.1971

— TRUE BLUE FACT —

Pompey have failed to beat Ipswich Town at Fratton Park since 1966.

Pompey players born on 3 September
Brian Bason b.1955;
John Charles Keyworth Curtis b.1978;
Lee Edward Russell b.1969;
Arthur (Archie) Styles b.1949

Pompey player born on 4 September
John Beresford b.1966

POMPEY PUB
The White House
Milton Road, Milton

Pompey players born on 5 September
John Armstrong b.1936;
Steven (Steve) Paul Bryant b.1953; Barry Ronald Cordjohn b.1942;
Martin MacDonald b.1931

Pomp & Posterity – 1967–68

Mike Trebilcock came to Fratton Park during this season to help Pompey gain promotion to the First Division but alas Pompey finished in fifth place.

Pompey players born on 6 September
David Best b.1943; Gerald (Gerry) Charles James Francis b.1951;
Henry Clifford (Cliff) Parker b.1913;
Malcolm Waldron b.1956

Pompey players born on 7 September
Garry Brady b.1976;
Arthur Egerton Knight b.1887

— STAR & CRESCENT HERO – PETER HARRIS —

Peter Harris is Pompey's most prolific goal scorer, netting 193 goals for the club in 479 League games. Not a bad return for a winger!

More than a goal scorer, though, Peter Harris was a local boy come good. Born in Portsea, he joined Pompey towards the end of the Second World War, and was a lynchpin in the back-to-back Championship-winning sides of 1949 and 1950. He won the respect of the fans for his loyalty and dedication to the club he loved and supported.

Peter's game was defined by his pace, goal-scoring ability and ball control. He was held by some in the same regard as such legends as Stanley Matthews and Tom Finney; however, unfortunately, his England career never really took off. He was capped twice by his country, making his debut in 1949 against Ireland, then made his final appearance four years later away to Hungary – a game in which England were on the receiving end of a 7–1 drubbing.

The highlights of his Pompey career include netting 33 goals during the two Championship seasons, and scoring seven hat-tricks – the first coming in a wartime match against S***hampton. His first peacetime hat-trick came against Stockport County in the FA Cup in a 7–0 win in 1949. In total he scored six hat-tricks and five in a 5–2 win over Aston Villa on 3 September 1958. Peter's final game was away in a 2–1 defeat at Rotherham on 21 November 1959. He was the club's top scorer in five separate seasons.

His Pompey career unfortunately ended prematurely in 1959 after a chest illness. However, Peter remained in the area and retired to Hayling Island.

Pompey players born on 8 September

Frederick John (Fred) Forward b.1899;
Robert (Robbie) John Pethick b.1970;
Jack Scholfield b.1902;
John Charles Trevor Smith b.1910;
Frederick J (Fred) Worrall b.1910

Pomp & Posterity – 1970–71

Norman Piper joined Pompey.

Pompey players born on 9 September

Christopher (Chris) Burns b.1967;
Rodney (Rod) Victor Taylor b.1943

— TRUE BLUE SONGS —

We'lllllllllllllllll drink a drink a drink
To Dave the Kemp a Kemp a Kemp
The saviour of the Portsmouth forward line
So we gave him a little white football
And now he's scoring all the time.

Sea, sea, seasiders
Sea, sea, seasiders
Sea, sea, seasiders.

Pompey players born on 10 September

Robert (Bobby) Nutley b.1916; Ian Edwin Stewart b.1961;
Thomas (Tommy) William James Taylor b.1946

— TO THE FRATTON FAITHFUL —

If you can't play on Fratton Park, you can't play anywhere.

Bobby Moore commenting on the quality of the Fratton Park pitch

Pompey players born on 11 September

John (Johnny) Duncan Sinclair Gordon b.1931;
Horace Leonard (Len) Phillips b.1922;
James Francis (Jim) Bellamy b.1881

— TRUE BLUE FACT —

Pompey lost 5–1 at home to Sheffield United in the league in 1969/70 and 1970/71 seasons.

Pompey players born on 12 September

Percy Albert Mark Cherrett b.1899;
Paul Andrew Smith b.1953;
David Anthony Thompson b.1977;
John Robert (Bob) Widdowson b.1941

Pomp & Posterity – 1972–73

John Deacon joined the Board, starting an association that would last 15 years.

Financial difficulties once again blighted the club despite the arrival of John Deacon in 1972. He went on to take full control in 1973, investing heavily in the club; however, things did not improve.

Pompey players born on 13 September

David Coid b.1891; Gary Lee Silk b.1984

— STAR & CRESCENT HERO – JIMMY SCOULAR —

Jimmy Scoular was discovered by Jack Tinn when he was assembling his Championship-winning side at the end of the Second World War. Spotted playing local football for Gosport Borough (Scoular was based at HMS *Dolphin* as a wartime engineer), the 20-year-old Scotsman was signed up in 1945.

Jimmy went on to become one of the key members of the Championship-winning sides of 1949 and 1950, and formed the formidable half-back line trio along with Jimmy Dickinson and Jack Froggatt.

It wasn't long before Scoular won admirers throughout the game as well as amongst the Fratton Park faithful. Indeed, the late Duncan Edwards regarded Scoular as 'the finest tackler of the ball I ever saw'. However, inevitably, along with his aggressive tackling came the occasional booking and sending off.

But there was more to Scoular's game than the tough tackling powerhouse, for he was equally renowned for skill and exquisite passing of the ball (he would even score the occasional goal). It was this that set him apart from the rest and made him a truly class player, and a Pompey legend. The surprise was that he was only capped nine times for Scotland during his stint at Fratton Park.

Scoular left the club for Newcastle in 1953 for a then significant fee of £26,000. He went from strength to strength in the North East, becoming Newcastle's captain and lifting the FA Cup with them in 1955.

Jimmy made 247 League appearances for Pompey, scoring on eight occasions, his first at Fratton Park on 20 March 1948 against Manchester City. He died in March 1998 aged 73.

Pompey players born on 14 September

George Randolph Lawrence b.1962;
Linvoy Stephen Primus b.1973

Pompey player born on 15 September
John Watson Fraser b.1938

Pomp & Posterity – 1973–74

John Deacon became Chairman and John Mortimore was appointed team manager.

Pompey player born on 16 September
George M Molyneuz b.1875

— STAR & CRESCENT HERO – ALAN KNIGHT —

Alan Knight, whose father was a Desert Rat serving in the famous British Eighth Army in the Second World War (under General Montgomery who would become a Director of Pompey), joined Pompey as a 16-year-old apprentice goalkeeper in 1978. The man who became known as 'the Legend' by Pompey fans went on to make 801 competitive appearances, the most made by a goalkeeper at a single club ever, in a career spanning 22 years. Knight is also the only Pompey player to have played in all four of the Football League divisions.

Alan supported West Ham as a kid and during his career West Ham manager Ron Greenwood once tried to sign him.

Knightsie picked up the nickname 'the Legend' from his teammates after he broke Peter Bonetti's record of most games played for one club in his 601st League game v Grimsby on 13 January 1996.

Knight's contribution to the club over his career was extensive; pulling off some amazing saves, he became known as a great shot-stopper and was Pompey's player of the year on three occasions (1981/82, 1994/95 and 1995/96).

Although he never made the full England squad, Knight was capped for the England youth team and the Under-21s. Knight retired in 2000 after 801 games. For his services to the community he was made a Member of the British Empire in 2001. Knight went on to work as goalkeeping coach at Pompey before departing and joining USA side FC Dallas.

ALAN SAID...

I remember thinking, as I hit the ground from my dive, 'I've saved it,' after getting a fingertip to the ball, then seeing it hit the inside of the post. I instinctively looked back, helpless as I watched the ball rolling back across me, inches from the goal-line. In almost slow-motion mode,

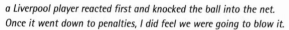

a Liverpool player reacted first and knocked the ball into the net. Once it went down to penalties, I did feel we were going to blow it.

On the FA Cup semi-final, 1992

The fans were absolutely unbelievable against Arsenal. The noise they made throughout the second half was such brilliant support. It struck a chord with the Arsenal players too, as Thierry Henry and Patrick Vieira came back on the pitch after the game to applaud our fans. For me, the most unique thing about the support was when Arsenal scored their fifth goal. You could not hear the Arsenal fans celebrate the goal as the entire Pompey crowd just upped the volume to drown out the away fans and get behind the boys.

After the Arsenal FA Cup defeat, 2004

I felt a sharp pain on the back of my neck, and went down as if I had been shot. It turned out to be a fruit pastille.

Our hero keeper's feelings of relief after falling victim to an object thrown from the crowd at Grimsby

...the England players and staff didn't seem to know who I was.

Alan Knight remembering his first England call-up

THEY SAID ABOUT ALAN...

He is incredibly old now and it seems he has been at Fratton Park as long as there has been a club.

Kit Symons on Knight's 800th appearance

I remember getting up in the mornings being greeted by Knightsie saying, 'We're in trouble.' It doesn't inspire confidence, does it!

Vince Hilaire, quoting his former team roommate

One day someone will work out the debt Pompey owe Alan Knight.

Pompey reporter Mike Neasom

He was a listener and a learner; when you make over 800 appearances, something must have been learned along the way.

Jeff Hemmerman

— ALAN KNIGHT'S (LEGEND) POMPEY XI —

Alan Knight (of course)

Warren Neil   Billy Gilbert   Andy Awford   Colin Sullivan

Vince Hilaire   Mick Kennedy   Mick Tait   Neil Webb

Paul Walsh   Mark Hateley

Subs: Kit Symons, Micky Quinn

ALAN KNIGHT ON HIS SELECTIONS

Colin Sullivan – because I see him now and again!

It was a toss-up between Awfs and Kit Symons but Awfs would get in because of his left foot.

I know there is no balance to this team, Vince Hilaire gets in ahead of Kevin O'Callaghan, and Mark Chamberlain would probably be injured and not available for selection.

Walshie was the best player I have played with in my time at Fratton Park for skill and ability.

As for Micky Quinn, he would be too fat to get off the bench. I saw him in a service station the other day and he was eating the whole place!

Pompey players born on 17 September

Kenneth George Ames b.1933; Michael (Mike) Christopher Fillery b.1960; David (Dave) Taylor b.1940

Pompey player born on 18 September

Sulzeer (Sol) Jeremiah Campbell b.1974

— TRUE BLUE FACT —

In 1973 Peter Marinello became Pompey's first £100,000 signing.

Pompey players born on 19 September

Christopher (Chris) Luke Tardif b.1979; Ognjen Koroman b.1978

Pomp & Posterity – 1974–75

John Mortimore was sacked and former Liverpool player Ian St John took over as Pompey manager.

The club were relegated to the Third Division the following season after finishing bottom in the table.

The season that followed saw Pompey only manage a 20th-place finish. In the season that followed, things deteriorated further when Pompey dropped down into the Fourth Division for the first time.

This low point for the club did, however, see a young goalkeeper make his first-team debut on that last game of the season. Alan Knight was the youngest first-team player ever.

Although now a Fourth Division club, Pompey still had a huge following and attracted record attendances up and down the country.

Pompey players born on 20 September

Sean Davis b.1979;
William (Billy) Alan Eames b.1957;
Stefani Miglioranzi b.1977;
Roy James Pack b.1976;
Michalis Vlachos b.1967

Pompey players born on 21 September

Ronald (Ron) Tudor Davies b.1932;
Rowan Lewis Vine b.1982

— TRUE BLUE FACTS —

Pompey were within five minutes of dropping to 92nd in the Football League until Steve Davey headed an equaliser at Hartlepool on 25 August 1978.

Pompey striker Benjani Mwaruwari used his BMW's sat-nav to try to reach the club's Fratton Park ground from London – and ended up in a builder's yard FIVE MILES away. The £4.1 million Zimbabwe star rang the club for directions.

1975–76 League Division Two

		P	W	D	L	F	A	W	D	L	F	A	Pts
1	Sunderland	42	19	2	0	48	10	5	6	10	19	26	56
2	Bristol City	42	11	7	3	34	14	8	8	5	25	21	53
3	WBA	42	10	9	2	29	12	10	4	7	21	21	53
4	Bolton W	42	12	5	4	36	14	8	7	6	28	24	52
5	Notts County	42	11	6	4	33	13	8	5	8	27	28	49
6	S***hampton	42	18	2	1	49	16	3	5	13	17	34	49
7	Luton Town	42	13	6	2	38	15	6	4	11	23	36	48
8	Nottingham Forest	42	13	1	7	34	18	4	11	6	21	22	46
9	Charlton Athletic	42	11	5	5	40	34	4	7	10	21	38	42
10	Blackpool	42	9	9	3	26	22	5	5	11	14	27	42
11	Chelsea	42	7	9	5	25	20	5	7	9	28	34	40
12	Fulham	42	9	8	4	27	14	4	6	11	18	33	40
13	Leyton Orient	42	10	6	5	21	12	3	8	10	16	27	40
14	Hull City	42	9	5	7	29	23	5	6	10	16	26	39
15	Blackburn Rovers	42	8	6	7	27	22	4	8	9	18	28	38
16	Plymouth Argyle	42	13	4	4	36	20	0	8	13	12	34	38
17	Oldham	42	11	8	2	37	24	2	4	15	20	44	38
18	Bristol Rovers	42	7	9	5	20	15	4	7	10	18	35	38
19	Carlisle Utd	42	9	8	4	29	22	3	5	13	16	37	37
20	Oxford Utd	42	7	7	7	23	25	4	4	13	16	34	33
21	York City	42	8	3	10	28	34	2	5	14	11	37	28
22	Pompey	42	4	6	11	15	23	5	1	15	17	38	25

Pompey players born on 22 September

John Frederick Moncur b.1966;
Robert C (Bob) Salmond b.1911;
Ronald (Ron) Albert Ernest Tindall b.1935

Pomp & Posterity – 1976–77

John Deacon appealed for public support, as a financial crisis hit the club – £20,000 was raised from the 'Save Our Soccer' organisation.

Ian St John was replaced as Pompey manager by Jimmy Dickinson.

Pompey players born on 23 September

Liam Sean Daish b.1968;
Arthur Holden b.1882

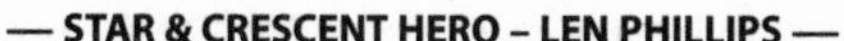

— STAR & CRESCENT HERO – LEN PHILLIPS —

Len Phillips was another of Pompey's back-to-back Championship-winning side. Jack Tinn, the legendary Pompey manager, spotted Phillips playing in the area for the Royal Marines and, impressed by what he saw, signed him up.

Possibly the greatest inside forward to play for the club, Phillips had a brilliant football brain. He was a crowd pleaser whose creativity could unlock any defence at his peak. He formed a prolific goal-scoring partnership with winger Peter Harris, scoring 11 (30 appearances) and 13 (37 appearances) in 1950–51 and 1951–52, respectively.

Destined for an international career, unfortunately for Phillips he only played for England three times (versus Northern Ireland, Wales and West Germany) after a knee injury ended his international career prematurely.

When Jimmy Scoular left for Newcastle, Phillips dropped into midfield where he continued to shine and could pick out the runs of Harris, forging a formidable relationship. Harris thrived on the precision service he received from Len – one of the reasons why Pompey were such a force in the early 1950s. After tearing a muscle ligament in an FA Cup tie against Grimsby in January 1956, Phillips turned to non-League for a while before scouting for Leeds United. Len remains a Pompey stalwart with a regular show of support at various supporters' events.

Pompey players born on 24 September

Petri Mikael Pasanen b.1980;
Mathias Svensson b.1975

Pompey player born on 25 September

Rudolphe Douala b.1978

Pompey players born on 26 September

John Robert Davies b.1933;
Alan Charles Stephenson b.1944

Pomp & Posterity – 1977–78

Despite a huge effort by the club's supporters, Pompey remained deep in financial trouble which was not helped by relegation to Division Four.

— STAR & CRESCENT HERO – RAY DANIEL —

Ray's big season for Pompey was the 1992/93 season, when promotion was so nearly achieved, only to lose out to West Ham on goals scored. Performing brilliantly at left-back that season, he was a popular choice for 'first-goal scorer' at the bookies.

Originally from Luton, Ray began his career at his hometown club. After spending a couple of years at Hull City, he moved on to Cardiff where he met up with Pompey manager-to-be Frank Burrows. After coming to Pompey, Frank brought Ray to Fratton Park in October 1990 for £80,000. Ray was 25 years old at the time.

After initially struggling to get in the team ahead of John Beresford, Ray's chance came after Beresford's transfer to Newcastle in the summer of 1992. His 40 League appearances in the following season helped Pompey come so close to promotion. His skill, pace and competent defending made him popular with the Fratton faithful.

Unfortunately, Ray found it hard to stay injury free and left the club in 1995 for Walsall.

Pompey players born on 27 September

Graham Robert Gaddes b.1941;
Arthur Goves b.1907;
Scot Patrick Hiley b.1968

— MEMORABLE GAMES —

Pompey v York City (Fratton Park)
14 May 1977
Result: 3–1
Pompey goal scorers: Green (2), Kemp

Under the guidance of the legendary Jimmy Dickinson and Ray Crawford, Pompey had to win this bottom-of-the-table clash to ease the threat of relegation to the Fourth Division. Shortly after the half-hour mark, York shocked the home fans by taking an unexpected lead but luckily this was short-lived with Pompey equalising through Clive Green.

Pompey came out the second half the better team and within 15 minutes of the restart were ahead through a Dave Kemp header.

Pompey's survival was guaranteed when Clive Green bagged his second and Pompey's third 18 minutes from the end.

1977–78 League Division Three													
		P	**W**	**D**	**L**	**F**	**A**	**W**	**D**	**L**	**F**	**A**	**Pts**
1	Wrexham	46	14	8	1	48	19	9	7	7	30	26	61
2	Cambridge	46	19	3	1	49	11	4	9	10	23	40	58
3	Preston NE	46	16	5	2	48	19	4	11	8	15	19	56
4	Peterborough Utd	46	15	7	1	32	11	5	9	9	15	22	56
5	Chester	46	14	8	1	41	24	2	14	7	18	32	54
6	Walsall	46	12	8	3	35	17	6	9	8	26	33	53
7	Gillingham	46	11	10	2	36	21	4	10	9	31	39	50
8	Colchester	46	10	11	2	36	16	5	7	11	19	28	48
9	Chesterfield	46	14	6	3	40	16	3	8	12	18	33	48
10	Swindon County	46	12	7	4	40	22	4	9	10	27	38	48
11	Shrewsbury Town	46	11	7	5	42	23	5	8	10	21	34	47
12	Tranmere Rovers	46	13	7	3	39	19	3	8	12	18	33	47
13	Carlisle Utd	46	10	9	4	32	26	4	10	9	27	33	47
14	Sheffield Wed	46	13	7	3	28	14	2	9	12	22	38	46
15	Bury	46	7	13	3	34	22	6	6	11	28	34	45
16	Lincoln City	46	10	8	5	35	26	5	7	11	18	35	45
17	Exeter City	46	11	8	4	30	18	4	6	13	19	41	44
18	Oxford Utd	46	11	10	2	38	21	2	4	17	26	46	40
19	Plymouth Argyle	46	7	8	8	33	28	4	9	10	28	40	39
20	Rotherham	46	11	5	7	26	19	2	8	13	25	49	39
21	Port Vale	46	7	11	5	28	23	1	9	13	18	44	36
22	Bradford City	46	11	6	6	40	29	1	4	18	16	57	34
23	Hereford	46	9	9	5	28	22	0	5	18	6	38	32
24	**Pompey**	**46**	**4**	**11**	**8**	**31**	**38**	**3**	**6**	**14**	**10**	**37**	**31**

Pompey player born on 28 September

John E (Jock) Gilfillan b.1898

Pompey players born on 29 September

William (Billy) Ernest Bevis b.1918;
Paul Gerard Cahill b.1955;
Andrew (Andy) Keith Petterson b.1969

Pompey players born on 30 September

Samuel (Sammy) Gary Igoe b.1975;
Michael (Mick) Paul Tait b.1956

— TRUE BLUE FACTS —

In the 1979/80 season, Pompey's average home League attendance in Division Four was nearly 16,000.

In 1927, Pompey gained promotion from Division Two ahead of third-place Manchester City on goal average (0.005 of a goal) even though City had scored 108 goals.

1979–80 League Division Four													
		P	**W**	**D**	**L**	**F**	**A**	**W**	**D**	**L**	**F**	**A**	**Pts**
1	Huddersfield	46	16	5	2	61	18	11	7	5	40	30	66
2	Walsall	46	12	9	2	43	23	11	9	3	32	24	64
3	Newport County	46	16	5	2	47	22	11	2	10	36	28	61
4	**Pompey**	**46**	**15**	**5**	**3**	**62**	**23**	**9**	**7**	**7**	**29**	**26**	**60**
5	Bradford City	46	14	6	3	44	14	10	6	7	33	36	60
6	Wigan Athletic	46	13	5	5	42	26	8	8	7	34	35	55
7	Lincoln	46	14	8	1	43	12	4	9	10	21	30	53
8	Peterborough	46	14	3	6	39	22	7	7	9	19	25	52
9	Torquay Utd	46	13	7	3	47	25	2	10	11	23	44	47
10	Aldershot	46	10	7	6	35	23	6	6	11	27	30	45
11	Bournemouth	46	8	9	6	32	25	5	9	9	20	26	44
12	Doncaster	46	11	6	6	37	27	4	8	11	25	36	44
13	Northampton	46	14	5	4	33	16	2	7	14	18	50	44
14	Scunthorpe	46	11	9	3	37	23	3	6	14	21	52	43
15	Tranmere Rovers	46	10	4	9	32	24	4	9	10	18	32	41
16	Stockport	46	9	7	7	30	31	5	5	13	18	41	40
17	York City	46	9	6	8	35	34	5	5	13	30	48	39
18	Halifax	46	11	9	3	29	20	2	4	17	17	52	39
19	Hartlepool	46	10	7	6	36	28	4	3	16	23	36	38
20	Port Vale	46	8	6	9	34	24	4	6	13	22	46	36
21	Hereford	46	8	7	8	22	21	3	7	13	16	31	36
22	Darlington	46	7	11	5	33	26	2	6	15	17	48	35
23	Crewe	46	10	6	7	25	27	1	7	15	10	41	35
24	Rochdale	46	6	7	10	20	28	1	6	16	13	51	27

Pompey players born on 1 October

Alexander (Alex) Reginald Totten b.1976;

Paul Anthony Walsh b.1962

Pomp & Posterity – 1978–79

Pompey in the League vault for the first time. At one point proud Pompey were 91st in the League. Just 30 years previously they had been League Division One Champions.

Pompey player born on 2 October

David Watson b.1900

— TRUE BLUE FACTS —

Full-back John McLaughlin scored on his debut at Hartlepool in 1979 but failed to find the net in his other 196 matches for the club.

In the 2001/2002 season, it was estimated that Pompey fans travelled 8,712 miles (average round trip – 371 miles) to watch Pompey on their travels!

Pompey players born on 3 October

James (Jim) Keith Brown b.1953;
Vincent de Paul Pericard b.1982;
John Douglas (Duggie) Jamieson Reid b.1917;
Edward Gordon Dundas Wright b.1884

POMPEY PUB

The Brewers Arms
Milton Road, Milton

Pompey player born on 4 October

Reginald Leonard (Len) Gundry b.1917

— TRUE BLUE FACT —

On 11 May 1979, Pompey played at Darlington in front of 1,140 fans, making this the lowest ever League attendance Pompey have played in front of.

Pompey players born on 5 October

Shaun David Cooper b.1983;
Brian Simon Horne b.1967;
David (Dave) Thomas b.1950

Pomp & Posterity – 1979–80

Pompey gained maximum points from their first five games. League attendances of up to 23,000 and 31,743 watched Pompey draw 1–1 with Middlesbrough in the FA Cup 3rd round. With promotion to Division Three, it looked like the club was on the comeback trail.

Pompey players born on 6 October

Harold (Harry) Buddery b.1889;
Brian Allan Edwards b.1930;
David Harry Gregory b.1951;
John (Jack) Martin b.1912

Pompey players born on 7 October

Colin Blant b.1946; John (Jack) Hogg b.1931;
George Smith b.1945;
Robert (Bob) Wallace b.1945

— TRUE BLUE FACT —

Goalkeeper Alan Knight holds the club record for a goalkeeper having been present in seasons 1982/83, 1984/85, 1986/87, 1989/90 and 1992/93.

Pompey players born on 8 October

Shaun Michael Gale b.1969;
Jeffery (Jeff) Hodgkins b.1942

Pompey player born on 9 October

Mikael (Mike) Panopoulos b.1976

Pompey players born on 10 October

Joseph W (Joe) Armstrong b.1882;
Vince Mark Hilaire b.1959;
Dean Laurence Kiely b.1970;
William (Willie) Morrison b.1939;
Ian James Gordon Neave b.1924;
Raymond (Ray) Pointer b.1936

1982–83 League Division Three													
		P	W	D	L	F	A	W	D	L	F	A	Pts
1	**Pompey**	46	16	4	3	43	19	11	6	6	31	22	91
2	Cardiff City	46	17	5	1	45	14	8	6	9	31	36	86
3	Huddersfield Town	46	15	8	0	56	18	8	5	10	28	31	82
4	Newport County	46	13	7	3	40	20	10	2	11	36	34	78
5	Oxford Utd	46	12	9	2	41	23	10	3	10	30	30	78
6	Lincoln City	46	17	1	5	55	22	6	6	11	22	29	76
7	Bristol Rovers	46	16	4	3	55	21	6	5	12	29	37	75
8	Plymouth Argyle	46	15	2	6	37	23	4	6	13	24	43	65
9	Brentford	46	14	4	5	50	28	4	6	13	38	49	64
10	Walsall	46	14	5	4	38	19	3	8	12	26	44	64
11	Sheffield Utd	46	16	3	4	44	20	3	4	16	18	44	64
12	Bradford City	46	11	7	5	41	27	5	6	12	27	42	61
13	Gillingham	46	12	4	7	37	29	4	9	10	21	30	61
14	Bournemouth	46	11	7	5	35	20	5	6	12	24	48	61
15	Southend Utd	46	10	8	5	41	28	5	6	12	25	37	59
16	Preston NE	46	11	10	2	35	17	4	3	16	25	52	58
17	Millwall	46	12	7	4	41	24	2	6	15	23	53	55
18	Wigan Athletic	46	10	4	9	35	33	5	5	13	25	39	54
19	Exeter City	46	12	4	7	49	43	2	8	13	32	61	54
20	Leyton Orient	46	10	6	7	44	38	5	3	15	20	50	54
21	Reading	46	10	8	5	37	28	2	9	12	27	51	53
22	Wrexham	46	11	6	6	40	26	1	9	13	16	50	51
23	Doncaster	46	6	8	9	38	44	3	3	17	19	53	38
24	Chesterfield	46	6	6	11	28	28	2	7	14	15	40	37

— MEMORABLE GAMES —

Liverpool v Pompey (Anfield)
28 October 1980
Result: 4–1
Pompey goal scorer: Kennedy (og)

This is a match remembered by many fans not for the result, but for the magnificent backing Pompey received for this evening game. When older fans reminisce about great games of the past in the pubs around Fratton Park, this match is invariably mentioned.

It's estimated more than 13,000 Pompey fans took over the Anfield Road End that night and outsang the legendary Liverpool Kop. As the players were lead out, the Pompey faithful decorated the evening sky with a blizzard of tickertape, a sight never to be forgotten.

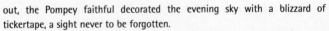

The game started and Pompey managed to hold their own until they conceded after 22 minutes. However, shortly before half-time, Pompey scored when Alan Kennedy turned an Alan Rogers cross into his own net, levelling the scores. Few present would disagree that this was the least Pompey's performance had deserved up until that point.

The joy was short-lived, however, as Johnson scored for Liverpool a minute later. It was a credit to Pompey that the score remained at 2–1 but on 80 minutes Johnson scored again. A late fourth for Liverpool from Souness ensured the scoreline was not a true reflection of the performance.

Pompey had given the League champions – a team including eight internationals – a run for their money. Combined with some special vocal support, this ensured that the game has gone down in Pompey folklore.

Pompey player born on 11 October
Jean-Francois (Jeff) Peron b.1965

— SEASON 1982–83 LEAGUE DIVISION 3 —

Date		Team	Result	Gate
28 Aug	A	Sheffield Utd	W 4–1	13361
04 Sept	A	Walsall	W 3–0	2922
08 Sept	A	Exeter City	W 3–0	3146
11 Sept	H	Wrexham	W 3–0	10867
18 Sept	A	Oxford	D 1–1	9918
25 Sept	H	Newport Co	L 1–2	10833
28 Sept	H	Millwall	W 2–0	7615
01 Oct	A	Southend	L 0–4	4589
09 Oct	A	Huddersfield	D 1–1	6243
16 Oct	H	Bournemouth	L 0–2	10961
19 Oct	A	Wigan	W 1–0	4504
23 Oct	H	Preston NE	W 3–1	10331
30 Oct	A	Cardiff	L 0–1	7082
02 Nov	H	Lincoln	W 4–1	12529
06 Nov	H	Gillingham	W 1–0	12212
13 Nov	A	Bristol R	L 1–5	9389
27 Nov	H	Doncaster	W 2–1	9474
04 Dec	A	Bradford City	D 2–2	4961
18 Dec	A	Chesterfield	W 1–0	2440

27 Dec	H	Brentford	W	2–1	14476
28 Dec	A	Reading	W	2–1	7646
01 Jan	H	Plymouth A	W	2–1	15856
15 Jan	A	Sheffield Utd	L	1–2	12907
18 Jan	A	Orient	L	1–2	3961
22 Jan	H	Oxford	W	1–0	10882
29 Jan	A	Reading	W	2–0	3007
06 Feb	A	Millwall	W	2–0	5621
12 Feb	H	Exeter	W	3–2	10622
16 Feb	A	Lincoln	W	3–0	6311
22 Feb	H	Huddersfield	W	3–2	18615
26 Feb	A	Bournemouth	W	2–0	13406
01 Mar	H	Wigan	D	0–0	16139
05 Mar	A	Preston NE	D	0–0	5610
12 Mar	H	Cardiff	D	0–0	24345
19 Mar	A	Gillingham	L	0–1	6489
26 Mar	H	Bristol R	W	1–0	17828
01 Apr	A	Brentford	D	1–1	12592
02 Apr	H	Reading	D	2–2	15327
09 Apr	H	Bradford	L	0–1	12198
23 Apr	A	Chesterfield	W	4–0	13003
30 Apr	A	Doncaster	W	2–0	2974
02 May	H	Orient	D	2–2	16232
07 May	H	Southend	W	2–0	18356
10 May	H	Walsall	W	1–0	22244
14 May	A	Plymouth A	W	1–0	14173

P46 W27 D10 L9 F74 A41 Pts 91
League Position 1st (promoted as Champions)

Appearances: A Knight, J McLaughlin, C Sullivan, R Doyle, E Howe, S Aizlewood, N Webb, M Tait, W Rafferty, A Biley, A Rogers, P Ellis, D Thomas, D Crown, T Senior, S Berry, T Ross, A Rollings, N Morgan, K Dillon. Manager: Bobby Campbell

Pompey players born on 12 October

Keven Francis Bartlett b.1962;
Allan Duncan Brown b.1926;
James (Jim) McCaffrey b.1951;
Paul Frank Went b.1949

Pomp & Posterity – 1980–84

Pompey were promoted back to Division Three and also became a Private Limited Company.

In the 1982/83 season, the club finished top of the Third Division. The 1980s saw a record signing in the form of Mark Hateley for £180,000. The England Under-21 striker provided the perfect strike partner for fans' favourite Alan Biley. Although the pair had no shortage of goals between them, the number of conceded goals left Pompey at the bottom end of the division once again.

Alan Ball arrived as manager in 1984.

— TRUE BLUE FACT —

In the 1983/4 season, Pompey scored more goals than Sheffield Wednesday (73 to 72) but Pompey finished 16th and Sheffield Wednesday were 2nd and were promoted.

Pompey players born on 13 October

Markus Heikkinen b.1978; Richard Money b.1955; Carl Philip Robinson b.1976

Pomp & Posterity – 1984–85

With 22 goals in 38 matches, including a goal for England against Brazil, Mark Hateley moved to AC Milan for £915,000, an offer that couldn't be refused.

Pompey narrowly missed promotion to the First Division when Manchester City took the promotion spot on goal difference.

Pompey player born on 14 October

Charles Robert Cooper b.1894

— STAR & CRESCENT HERO – DARREN ANDERTON —

Darren Anderton was a product of the Pompey youth team and made his first-team debut at home against Wolverhampton Wanderers on 3 November 1990. Most fans will remember Anderton's contribution to the famous FA Cup run of 1992. He played a huge part in reaching the semi-finals against Liverpool, by scoring twice in each of the previous rounds against Leyton Orient and the replay away at Middlesbrough. After beating Nottingham Forest 1–0 at Fratton Park, Pompey were drawn against Liverpool at Highbury and it was an Anderton goal in the second period of extra-time which sent the Pompey fans into a frenzy only to be brought down to earth with a bump when Whelan equalised with four minutes to go. Pompey lost the subsequent replay at Villa Park eight days later and it was not long after the season finished that Anderton left Pompey for Spurs for an estimated £1.7 million.

Pompey players born on 15 October
Andrew (Andy) Alexander Cole b.1971;
Steven (Steve) Wigley b.1961

Pomp & Posterity – 1985–87

1985/86 – Pompey fell short of promotion by three points.

1986/87 – Pompey won promotion to Division One after finishing in second place. The club achieved 14 successive home wins and returned to the top flight of English football for the first time in 27 years.

Pompey players born on 16 October
James Phillips (Jimmy) Allen b.1909;
John Michael Beale b.1930;
David Gerald Unsworth b.1973

Pompey players born on 17 October
John (Jack) Froggatt b.1922;
Clifford (Cliff) Portwood b.1937

Pomp & Posterity – 1987–88

John Deacon's massive effort in terms of financial support ended in disappointment and relegation. Many fans saw the sale of Mick Kennedy as a big factor. In a season of few high points, beating S***hampton at the Dell on 3 January 1988 became such a legendary day that a fanzine was named after the event.

After John Deacon's dream of First Division football was so short-lived, he sold up to Jim Gregory in the summer of 1988.

— SEASON 1986–87 LEAGUE DIVISION 2 —

Date		Team	Result	Gate
23 Aug	A	Brighton	D 0–0	13723
30 Aug	H	Ipswich	D 1–1	11849
02 Sept	A	Hull	W 2–0	7706
06 Sept	A	Barnsley	W 2–0	4341
13 Sept	H	Blackburn	W 1–0	8733
20 Sept	A	Stoke	D 1–1	8440
27 Sept	H	Huddersfield	W 1–0	9022
04 Oct	A	Sunderland	D 0–0	16938
11 Oct	H	Birmingham	W 2–0	11252
18 Oct	A	Leeds	L 1–3	21361
21 Oct	H	Derby	W 3–1	9131
25 Oct	H	WBA	W 2–1	11608
01 Nov	A	Oldham	D 0–0	8635
08 Nov	H	Bradford C	W 2–1	10027
15 Nov	A	Shrewsbury	L 0–1	3827
22 Nov	H	Grimsby	W 2–1	9517
29 Nov	A	Millwall	D 1–1	5031
06 Dec	H	C Palace	W 2–0	10907
13 Dec	A	Sheffield Utd	L 0–1	9523
20 Dec	H	Barnsley	W 2–1	9568
26 Dec	A	Plymouth A	W 3–2	21249
29 Dec	H	Shrewsbury	W 3–0	15006
01 Jan	H	Reading	W 1–0	18289
03 Jan	A	Blackburn	L 0–1	6582
24 Jan	H	Brighton	W 1–0	12992
07 Feb	A	Ipswich	W 1–0	18670
14 Feb	H	Hull	W 1–0	11098
21 Feb	A	Huddersfield	L 0–2	6229
28 Feb	H	Stoke	W 3–0	14607
04 Mar	A	Derby	D 0–0	21085
10 Mar	H	Leeds	D 1–1	13745
21 Mar	A	Birmingham	W 1–0	9823
28 Mar	H	Sunderland	W 3–1	13371
04 Apr	A	Bradford C	L 0–1	8570
11 Apr	H	Oldham	W 3–0	19708
18 Apr	A	Reading	D 2–2	9549
20 Apr	H	Plymouth	L 0–1	17171
27 Apr	A	Grimsby	W 2–0	5085

29 Apr	A	WBA	L 0–1	10007
02 May	H	Millwall	W 2–0	15777
04 Mar	A	C Palace	L 0–1	18029
09 Mar	H	Sheffield Utd	L 1–2	28001

P42 W23 D9 L10 F53 A28 Pts 78
League Position 2nd (Promoted)

Appearances: A Knight, B Gilbert, K Ball, N Blake, E Collins, L Daish, K Dillon, B Gilbert, P Hardyman, V Hilaire, M Kennedy, P Mariner, N Morgan, K O'Callaghan, M Quinn, K Russell, K Swain, M Tait, M Thomas, P Wood

1986–87 League Division Two

		P	W	D	L	F	A	W	D	L	F	A	Pts
1	Derby County	42	14	6	1	42	18	11	3	7	22	20	84
2	**Pompey**	**42**	**17**	**2**	**2**	**37**	**11**	**6**	**7**	**8**	**16**	**17**	**78**
3	Oldham Athletic	42	13	6	2	36	16	9	3	9	29	28	75
4	Leeds Utd	42	15	4	2	43	16	4	7	10	15	28	68
5	Ipswich Town	42	12	6	3	29	10	5	7	9	30	33	64
6	Crystal Palace	42	12	4	5	35	20	7	1	13	16	33	62
7	Plymouth Argyle	42	12	6	3	40	23	4	7	10	22	34	61
8	Stoke City	42	11	5	5	40	21	5	5	11	23	32	58
9	Sheffield Utd	42	10	8	3	31	19	5	5	11	19	30	58
10	Bradford City	42	10	5	6	36	27	5	5	11	26	35	55
11	Barnsley	42	8	7	6	26	23	6	6	9	23	29	55
12	Blackburn Rovers	42	11	4	6	30	22	4	6	11	15	33	55
13	Reading	42	11	4	6	33	23	3	7	11	19	36	53
14	Hull City	42	10	6	5	25	22	3	8	10	16	33	53
15	West Brom	42	8	6	7	29	22	5	6	10	22	27	51
16	Millwall	42	10	5	6	27	16	4	4	13	12	29	51
17	Huddersfield	42	9	6	6	38	30	4	6	11	16	31	51
18	Shrewsbury	42	11	3	7	24	14	4	3	14	17	39	51
19	Birmingham City	42	8	9	4	27	21	3	8	10	20	38	50
20	Sunderland	42	8	6	7	25	23	4	6	11	24	36	48
21	Grimsby Town	42	5	8	8	18	21	5	6	10	21	38	44
22	Brighton HA	42	7	6	8	22	20	2	6	13	15	34	39

Pompey players born on 18 October

James (Jim) Forsyth b.1904;

John Jarvie b.1900

Pompey player born on 19 October

Kevin O'Callaghan b.1961

— TRUE BLUE FACT —

Apart from playing in goal, Mick Tait played in every position during his seven-year spell with the club, 1980–87.

Pompey player born on 20 October

Christopher (Chris) Lawler b.1943

1987–88 League Division One

		P	W	D	L	F	A	W	D	L	F	A	Pts
1	Liverpool	40	15	5	0	49	9	11	7	2	38	15	90
2	Man Utd	40	14	5	1	41	17	9	7	4	30	21	81
3	Nottingham Forest	40	11	7	2	40	17	9	6	5	27	22	73
4	Everton	40	14	4	2	34	11	5	9	6	19	16	70
5	QPR	40	12	4	4	30	14	7	6	7	18	24	67
6	Arsenal	40	11	4	5	35	16	7	8	5	23	23	66
7	Wimbledon	40	8	9	3	32	20	6	6	8	26	27	57
8	Newcastle Utd	40	9	6	5	32	23	5	8	7	23	30	56
9	Luton Town	40	11	6	3	40	21	3	5	12	17	37	53
10	Coventry City	40	6	8	6	23	25	7	6	7	23	28	53
11	Sheffield Wed	40	10	2	8	27	30	5	6	9	25	36	53
12	S***hampton	40	6	8	6	27	26	6	6	8	22	27	50
13	Tottenham Hotspur	40	9	5	6	26	23	3	6	11	12	25	47
14	Norwich City	40	7	5	8	26	26	5	4	11	14	26	45
15	Derby County	40	6	7	7	18	17	4	6	10	17	28	43
16	West Ham	40	6	9	5	23	21	3	6	11	17	31	42
17	Charlton Athletic	40	7	7	6	23	21	2	8	10	15	31	42
18	Chelsea	40	7	11	2	24	17	2	4	14	26	51	42
19	**Pompey**	**40**	**4**	**8**	**8**	**21**	**27**	**3**	**6**	**11**	**15**	**39**	**35**
20	Watford	40	4	5	11	15	24	3	6	11	12	27	32
21	Oxford Utd	40	5	7	8	24	34	1	6	13	20	46	31

Pompey player born on 21 October

George Haslam b.1898

— TO THE FRATTON FAITHFUL —

Hoo-lay, Hoo-lay, Hoo-lay-gan...

The 1980s saw an increase in football hooliganism and Pompey had the '657' Crew, named after the 6.57 train they used to catch to travel to away games. By the start of the 1990s and the introduction of all-seater stadiums, football-related violence had decreased dramatically.

Pompey players born on 22 October

Eamonn Anthony Stephen Collins b.1965;
David (Dave) John Leworthy b.1962

— TRUE BLUE FACT —

Pompey fans have been banned from watching their team due to various reasons at Millwall (1985, 1986, 2003), Luton (1988), Bradford (1985) and all reserve matches at S***hampton since winning promotion to the Premiership.

Pompey players born on 23 October

Robert Muir b.1910; Jasper Herbert Yeuell b.1925

POMPEY PUB

The Magpie
Fratton Road, Portsmouth

Pompey players born on 24 October

Richard (Dick) Scott Beattie b.1978; Patrick (Pat) Thomas Neil b.1937

— STAR & CRESCENT HERO – STEVE CLARIDGE —

Steve Claridge had a long and varied career. As a local lad, he started his apprenticeship at Pompey in 1982. It was felt, however, that he would not make the grade and he was released to Fareham Town.

The following years saw Steve move around a great deal, and his clubs included Bournemouth – where he was released by then manager Harry Redknapp – Weymouth, Crystal Palace, Aldershot and Cambridge United.

It was at Cambridge where Steve briefly came to the attention of Pompey fans again during the final game of the 1992/93 season. Pompey were at home, needing to better West Ham's score by two goals to guarantee promotion to the Premiership. West Ham were away to Cambridge and facing one Steve Claridge.

As Pompey struggled to overcome a stubborn Grimsby side, before eventually winning 2–1, all ears were on the Abbey Stadium where Steve managed to score two goals, only for them both to be ruled offside. This caused much confusion on the terraces back at Fratton Park where fans were relying on crackling hand-held radios. Ultimately, it was not to be, though, and Pompey subsequently failed in the play-offs.

Fast forward to January 1998 and Steve returned to his hometown club on loan. Along with Alan Ball, Steve inspired the club to another great escape from relegation, and efforts were made to sign him permanently in the close season. The transfer fee could not be matched, however, and he signed for Wolves. His short spell proved unsuccessful, though, and he finally joined Pompey permanently for a reduced fee in time for the 1998/99 season.

The next three seasons saw Steve cement his place as a fans' favourite, winning the player of the year award two seasons running. In October 2000, Pompey and Tony Pulis went their separate ways, and, surprisingly, Steve was appointed player-manager. After a bright start, with three consecutive wins, results dipped a little, and Graham Rix was controversially appointed manager in February 2001.

Steve went on to have a successful spell at Millwall before moving into management at Weymouth.

Pompey players born on 25 October

Deon John Burton b.1976;
Ivor James Evans b.1933; George (Garth) Hudson b.1923;
Gary Macdonald b.1979; Zillwood George (Zack) March b.1892;
Lee Tierling b.1972

— TRUE BLUE SONGS —

In Portsmouth's fair city,
Where the girls are so pretty,
I first set my eyes on sweet Molly Malone
She wheeled her wheelbarrow,
Through streets wide and narrow,
Singing da da da da da da da da da Portsmouth.

We all follow the Portsmouth
Over land and sea and Sainsbury's
We all follow the Portsmouth wherever they may be ...
Altogether now.

Pompey player born on 26 October
Donald (Don) Simon Colombo b.1928

Pompey players born on 27 October
Roger Davidson b.1948; Adrian Richard Whitbread b.1971

— TRUE BLUE FACT —

Colin Clarke, David Seaman and Paul Walsh all had their careers ended on the Fratton Park pitch by injury.

Pompey players born on 28 October
Stuart James Doling b.1972;
Dejan Stefanovic b.1974

— TO THE FRATTON FAITHFUL —

Guy the Guy

The start of the 1990s saw the emergence of a new hero at Fratton Park in the form of Guy Whittingham who, after buying himself out of the army, went on to break the scoring record at the club previously set by Billy Haines.

Pompey players born on 29 October
Leigh Kenneth Barnard b.1958;
John McLaughlin b.1954;
Andrew (Andy) Couper Stewart b.1956;
Alexander (Alex) Wilson b.1933

Pomp & Posterity – 1991–92

Jim Smith appointed as manager; he had previously worked under Gregory at Queens Park Rangers.

Pompey players born on 30 October
Guy Butters b.1969; Colin John Clarke b.1962;
James (Jimmy) Clugston b.1934;
Nicholas (Nicky) Morgan b.1959;
Mark Summerbee b.1976

— THE ILLUSTRIOUS JAMES SMITH ESQ. —
(*LEGENDARI BALDMOSTOS*)

JIM SMITH SAID...

Portsmouth was a big club and I was anxious to put it back on the map and I felt that this time I would be given the support I needed to try and do that.

On joining Pompey

I can't say that it was a 'hair-raising experience.'
I didn't lose my hair, I just grew through it.
I prefer a wide parting.

On being 'follicle changed'

Vincent Pericard is the unofficial interpreter. I speak to Vincent in English, he tells the others in French. Only problem is I can't actually know what he is telling them.

The Old Bald Eagle's communication policy

We make it difficult for ourselves at times – and exciting for everyone else.

Following a match with Preston in 2002

Anderton has been a somewhat unlucky player in recent years, sustaining a number of injuries which have earned him the rather caustic nickname of 'Sicknote.' But fully fit and on his day, there are not many better or more honest players around.

On Darren Anderton

I decided to leave nothing to chance in our preparation for the game – even to the extent of taking in a local Sunday church service on the morning of the match. But just to be on the safe side we also attended to the more earthly matters of devising a game plan that I felt could expose Liverpool at the back where I believed they tended to play very square.

On the Liverpool semi-final, 1992

I have to say I went raving mad in the dressing room afterwards and I remember telling the players, 'This result will come back and give us sleepless nights' – and it did.

Looking back, the most remarkable game was the 5–5 draw at Oxford. Particularly poignant for me being an Oxford lad and ex-manager. It got to 5–2 and I thought, 'No more, don't want to embarrass them.' With 13 minutes left, they got one, then another. The lads know, if they put it out from kick-off, the ref will blow for time. We made the mistake of passing back to Maguire, probably the worst thing we could do. He boots it up field to their goalkeeper who kicks it the length of the field and seconds later it's 5–5. I said to the lads, 'This will haunt you the rest of your lives.' By the end of the season, those two points cost us a place in the Premiership.

The Bald Eagle's Memorable Game: Oxford 5 Pompey 5

Pompey players born on 31 October
Keith Michael George East b.1944;
Ricardo Dwayne Fuller b.1979;
John Ernest Lovett b.1940;
Maitland (Matt) Alexander Inglis Pollock b.1953

— MEMORABLE GAMES —

FA Cup Semi-final (Highbury)
Pompey v Liverpool
5 April 1992
Result: 1–1
Pompey goal scorer: Anderton

A fantastic FA Cup run saw Pompey in the semi-finals facing Liverpool after overcoming the likes of Exeter, Leyton Orient, Middlesbrough and finally Nottingham Forest with a goal after two minutes from 'on loan' striker Alan McLoughlin. Pompey managed to hang on for a 1–0 victory prompting the headline 'SOMETHING BORROWED, SOMETHING BLUE'.

Nearly 20,000 Pompey fans packed out the Clock End at Highbury for a game that produced deeply mixed emotions for the Pompey faithful.

Darren Anderton put the Blues ahead with eight minutes to go, sparking a goal celebration that all present would find difficult to top. Pompey were just three minutes and 42 seconds away from their first FA Cup Final appearance since 1939, but sadly Andy Awford fouled Steve Nichol 25 yards from goal. The resultant John

Barnes free-kick forced Alan Knight into a fingertip save, but the rebound off the post was turned in by Ronnie Whelan.

Pompey had matched Liverpool for 90 minutes, forcing extra-time.

At the start of the second half of extra-time, Darren Anderton scored, sending the Pompey fans wild, only for them to look on in horror when four minutes from time Liverpool equalised through Ronnie Whelan.

Further heartbreak was to follow a week later when the replay at Villa Park saw a heroic performance unrewarded after the Blues crashed out of a penalty shoot-out after extra-time.

Despite the disappointment, some fans have pointed to these games, and the promotion near-miss the following season, as helping to attract a new younger generation of fans to the club.

Pompey players born on 1 November

Cecil (Archie) James Andrews b.1930;
William (Willie) Macaulay b.1879;
Albert McCann b.1941; Paolo Andrea Pietro Vernazza b.1979;
Paul Anthony Wood b.1964;
George Frederick (Fred) Wheldon b.1869

— TRUE BLUE FACT —

Pompey have never got past the quarter-final stage of the League Cup.

Pompey players born on 2 November

Derek Harold (Harry) Harris b.1933; Stephen (Steve) Piper b.1953

Pomp & Posterity – 1992–93

Pompey were denied Premiership status by two goals when losing out in the play-off semi-finals to Leicester City by way of a goal that the referee himself later called 'dubious'.

Guy 'Corporal Punishment' Whittingham scored 42 League goals in a single season, to take the long-established record of Billy 'Farmer's Boy' Haines. Paul Walsh arrived at Fratton Park and was to become a fantastic partner to Guy Whittingham. Pompey narrowly missed an automatic promotion spot to West Ham. The play-offs led to disappointment when, despite finishing 12 points behind Pompey, Leicester gained promotion. The end of the season saw the departure of Guy Whittingham.

— STAR & CRESCENT HERO – PAUL WALSH —

Paul Walsh has to be one of the most exciting players ever to play for Pompey. Some of his performances in the 1992–93 season were outstanding, and at that time he was clearly in a different class in the second tier of English football.

Following the sale of Darren Anderton to Tottenham in the summer of 1992, Jim Smith managed to tempt Paul to the south coast for a fee of £400,000. He went straight into the team for the opening game of the season and immediately struck up an understanding with Guy Whittingham who bagged a hat-trick on the opening day.

Although he was not a prolific goal scorer during that season, many of Whittingham's 42 goals were made by Walsh. His close control and trickery were too much for many defenders in the division. His work rate was also second to none – something which is always appreciated by the Fratton Park crowd.

Paul's career before he joined Pompey could be described as 'unfulfilled potential'. Starting his career at Charlton, he won England youth honours in the early 1980s before transferring to Luton Town in 1982. He was Luton's top scorer in the 1983–84 season, and won five full England caps while at Luton before being snapped up by Liverpool for £700,000.

This is when injury started to blight Paul's career. However, while at Liverpool, he featured in the European Cup Final at the Heysel Stadium in 1985. He also featured in the Double-winning side of 1985–86, weighing in with 11 goals in 20 appearances. But, again, appearances were limited by continuing injury problems.

After the promotion near-miss in the 1992–93 season, the 1993–94 season was somewhat less exciting, and Paul was sold to Manchester City in April 1994 for £750,000. Again, Paul became a fans' favourite at City before re-signing for Pompey late in 1995 in exchange for Gerry Creaney.

Sadly, Paul's career came to an end in February 1996 after he suffered a knee injury playing against Leicester at Fratton Park.

Pompey player born on 3 November

Andrew (Andy) John Myers b.1973

Pompey players born on 4 November

George Alan Samuel Barnett b.1944;

Roy Evan Lunniss b.1939;

Thomas (Tom) Maidment b.1905

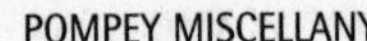

— TO THE FRATTON FAITHFUL —

Since I left Portsmouth I've played about 15 charity games and I am still waiting for a pass from Paul Walsh! It is unbelievable trying to get a pass from him!

Vince Hilaire

Pompey player born on 5 November
John Robson Weddle b.1905

— TRUE BLUE FACT —

Pompey have drawn 5–5 just once in their history at Oxford United in 1992.

Pompey players born on 6 November
Henry Clifford (Cliff) Parker b.1913;
Ronald (Ron) Saunders b.1932;
Paul Anthony Sugrue b.1960

Pomp & Posterity – 1994–96

Pompey finished a disappointing 17th in the League. Fans were left reeling in 1995 with the shock sacking of Jim Smith who was replaced by Terry Fenwick.

1995/96 – the relegation battle continued right to the last game of the season. Pompey managed a win at Huddersfield and survived the drop on goal difference condemning Millwall to Division Two. There was no FA Cup run to cheer the fans up; in fact, the opposite was the case when Pompey got drawn at rivals S***hhampton in the 3rd round and lost 3–0.

Jim Smith was now managing Derby County and, while relegation was only just avoided at Pompey, Smith and Derby achieved promotion to the Premier League.

Following months of speculation, Terry Venables finally arrived at Fratton Park as Chairman in 1996 after leaving his position as England coach after Euro '96. In the second half of their programme, Pompey began to show some quality and took a notable FA Cup scalp at Leeds. Pompey just failed to claim a play-off place.

— STAR & CRESCENT HERO – LINVOY PRIMUS —

Linvoy is another player that has gained cult-hero status amongst the fans. It seems that most seasons a new defender is signed or an existing player starts the season ahead of Linvoy, but time after time he gains back his spot in the starting line-up and turns in the sort of displays which makes you wonder why he was ever left out in the first place.

Linvoy joined Pompey in the summer of 2000 after having previously played for Charlton, Barnet and Reading. Tony Pulis shrewdly signed him on a free transfer as he was out of contract with Reading at the time. After initially suffering with injury problems, Linvoy went on to develop a strong partnership with Darren Moore. Although Moore was arguably the higher-profile player at that time, Linvoy's steady performances did not go unnoticed.

Strong in the air, and not short of pace, Linvoy has gone on to play against some of the best strikers in the world and prove more than a match for them, winning accolades from the likes of Thierry Henry.

Since signing, Linvoy has won many fans' awards, and is very well thought of throughout the city for his loyalty and attitude and for all the voluntary work he does in the community.

Pompey players born on 7 November

Kenneth (Ken) Taylor Foggo b.1943;
Mark Wayne Hateley b.1961

Pompey players born on 8 November

Andrew (Andy) Robert Gosney b.1963;
Peter Higham b.1930;
Roger Jones b.1946

—TRUE BLUE FACT —

Pompey drew 4–4 with AEK Athens in the Thrace Cup in Greece at the end of the 1993–94 season and went on to win 5–4 on penalties having been 4–0 down with 12 minutes remaining.

Pompey players born on 9 November

Stephen Mark Agnew b.1965;
Keith Allen b.1943;
James (Jimmy) William Charles Carter b. 1965;
Terence (Terry) Fitzroy Connor b.1962;
Jeffrey (Jeff) King b.1953;
Maurice Peter Leather b.1929

Pomp & Posterity – 1997–98

By the 1997/98 season, Venables was also in a management role with the Australia national team, a move which saw several Australian players arrive at Fratton Park, the most successful of them being John Aloisi. October 1997 saw the opening of the new 'Fratton End' which restored this part of the ground to its former size from a decade before.

After a poor start Pompey sacked Fenwick. On the last day of the season Pompey won 3–1 at Bradford to save their First Division status. On their desperate run to stay up, Pompey beat Stockport 1–0 in a match which became known for the 'wall of sound' that came from the fans.

Alan Ball returned as manager in 1998 and he managed to acquire Steve Claridge on loan from Leicester City, who went on to become not only a permanent fixture but also a fans' favourite and, ultimately, but briefly, Pompey manager. The end of that season saw yet another relegation nail-biter as Pompey travelled to Bradford.

Pompey players born on 10 November

Patrik Berger b.1973;
William (Billy) Albert Gilbert b.1959;
Guy Whittingham b.1964

— TRUE BLUE FACT —

Pompey went 11 matches without a win from September to November 1997.

Pompey player born on 11 November

Francis Raymond (Frank) O'Connor b.1912

— TO THE FRATTON FAITHFUL —

Handed a bookies pen to write down a phone number, Steve Claridge scribbled away without any ink coming out. Looking up, a lamenting Claridge said, 'I wish it hadn't worked in the past.'

Pompey players born on 12 November
Kevin Anthony Ball b.1964; Jason Victor Cundy b.1969;
Harold (Harry) Foxall b.1901; Brendan John O'Connell b.1966

Pompey player born on 13 November
Paul Philip Wimbleton b.1964

— A POEM BY NEIL WEBB, EX-POMPEY, FOREST AND ENGLAND —

Play up Pompey – you've made it to the top at last,
Not that I ever doubted that this would come to pass.
For with fans so loyal and faithful, through all the sweat and tears,
If anyone deserves success, then 1987 is your year.

So it's off to Manchester United, Liverpool and Spurs,
And to me at Forest – will it bring you down to earth?
Although I shouldn't say it, I hope we draw three all,
With me scoring a hat-trick and Ballie presenting the ball!

Pompey player born on 14 November
Michael (Mick) Anthony Mellows b.1947

— MEMORABLE GAMES —

Bradford City v Pompey (Valley Parade)
3 May 1998
Result: 1–3
Pompey goal scorers: Durnin (2), Igoe
Pompey travelled to Valley Parade on the final game of the season needing a win to ensure survival in the First Division. Relegated at Pompey's expense would be Stoke and Manchester City.

Around 4,000 Pompey fans made the trip to Valley Parade. Nerves were shredded during the early part of the first half, as Bradford started the better team, and rattled the crossbar from a free-kick. However, John Durnin put the Blues ahead on 35 minutes against the run of play.

The second half saw an onslaught on the Pompey goal, with Aaron Flahavan turning in a man-of-the-match performance to keep the Blues in it. Then, again against the run of play, Sammy Igoe scored a blinder from 25 yards. Then, incredibly, John Durnin headed home again from a Robbie Pethick cross nine minutes later.

The travelling faithful could now start the celebrations as Bradford could only muster a late consolation goal. The final whistle saw a pitch invasion from both sets of fans, as the Bradford contingent decided to join the party and have a laugh at the expense of near rivals Manchester City.

Pompey player born on 15 November
Boris Zivkovic b.1975

— TO THE FRATTON FAITHFUL —

Frustration

The latter part of the 1990s saw fans increasingly frustrated with the Gregory family and the way the club was being run. It was during this time the club was on the verge of going into administration unless a buyer was found. Thankfully, in 1999, after several false dawns, this buyer came in the form of Serbian/American millionaire Milan Mandaric.

Pompey player born on 16 November
David Thackeray b.1900

— TRUE BLUE FACT —

At Swindon in 21 February 1999, Pompey fans were given both ends of the ground (approx. 4,000 travelled that day).

Pompey player born on 17 November
Brian Carter b.1938

POMPEY PUB
The Travellers Joy
Milton Road, Milton

Pompey player born on 18 November
John (Jack) Platt b.1880

Pomp & Posterity – 1998–99

Pompey appointed Alan Ball as manager for the second time.

Last-day drama at Bradford saved the club from relegation. Milan Mandaric rescued Pompey from closure.

Pompey players born on 19 November
Wilfred (Wilf) Blackwell b.1926;
Mark Valentine Chamberlain b.1961;
Paul Graham Harries b.1977

— STAR & CRESCENT HERO – MICKY QUINN —

Michael 'Micky' Quinn was born on the Cantril Farm estate in Liverpool of Irish and Italian descent. A fine centre-forward and a consistent goal-getter, he was also noted for his ample proportions. The coupling of these two observations gave rise to the terrace song 'He's fat, he's round, he scores at every ground, Mick Quinn!' A variation of this was often heard during his time at Fratton Park: 'He's fat, he's round, he's worth a million pounds!'

Not known for his skilful play outside the box, it was his work in the penalty area that made Mick a favourite with the Pompey faithful.

On hearing that Jack Charlton was looking at scouser Quinn for the Irish Republic, Mick was quoted as saying, 'My mum has got an Irish wolfhound, perhaps that is how I qualify.'

And he did.

Quinn started his career as an apprentice with Derby County, but he turned professional with Wigan Athletic in September 1979. He made his League debut with the Latics at the age of 17. After a spell with Stockport County from June 1982 he moved to Oldham Athletic in January 1984. At Boundary Park, Mick averaged a goal a game.

Quinn joined Pompey in March 1986. Alan Ball, the manager of Pompey at the time, was set to sign Andy Ritchie from Leeds; however, a knee injury at the last minute caused the deal to collapse. Two days later, Ball signed Mick, then 23 years old, for a fee of £150,000.

Quinn finished the season as Pompey's leading goal scorer during the club's Second Division promotion campaign, despite spending two weeks of that season banged up in prison for a driving offence (he was also disqualified from driving). He had been caught driving twice after receiving a ban for drink-driving. But Quinney was well loved by the fans at Fratton Park and, as his goals seemed to go in 'two by two', he was nicknamed 'Noah'.

Pompey were pushing for promotion to the First Division, but ultimately fell short. Even so, Mick still managed to score six goals in 11 outings that season. It was, however, in the following promotion season of 1986/87 where Mick made his name, firing Pompey into the First Division as leading scorer. He netted 22 times in 39 League appearances that season.

Despite this performance, manager Alan Ball had doubts about his ability to make it in the top flight and accepted an offer of £300,000 from Millwall for his services. Mick decided to stay and fight for his place, and, although he made 29 appearances, he only managed six goals in the First Division. This was of course in a struggling team that was ultimately relegated after one season in the top flight.

In July 1989, Mick went to Newcastle United for £650,000, following the Magpies' relegation to the Second Division. On his debut for the club, he scored four goals against Leeds United and finished the season top goal scorer in the Second Division, netting 34 times. However, the North-Easterners missed out on an automatic promotion place; Leeds United and Sheffield United went up, and Newcastle stayed down, after losing to Swindon Town in the play-offs.

Quinn moved to Coventry City in 1992 and, in his first six months at Highfield Road, he hit 17 Premiership goals – 10 of them in his initial half-a-dozen outings. But Mick's efforts couldn't pull the Sky Blues further than 15th place by the conclusion of their schedule. The following season saw the club improve by four places, helped by Quinn's regular contributions. During the 1993–94 season, Mick continued to score goals, but in September 1994 Coventry signed Dion Dublin and it became clear that it was time for the Mighty Quinn to move on.

Following uneventful loan periods with Plymouth Argyle (November 1994) and Watford (March 1995), Mick moved to PAOK Salonika.

After what proved to be a short stay in Greece, in 1996 Quinn was amongst the applicants for the manager's job at Burnley. However, Adrian Heath took the hot-seat at Turf Moor, and Mick decided to make the move away from football and concentrate on his career as a racehorse trainer.

In August 2001, Quinn was suspended from racehorse training for two-and-a-half years; the RSPCA had discovered that three of his racehorses had been badly neglected. However, on appeal, this ban was reduced to 12 months.

In 2003, Mick's autobiography *Who Ate All The Pies?* hit the shelves and is one of the better reads amongst the often undistinguished genre that is football-related literature. Two years later, Quinn signed a contract with the *Cambridge Evening News* to write a column entitled 'Who Ate All The Pies?' commenting on football, sport and the world in general.

In 2006, Mick was one of the stars of the TV series *Celebrity Fit Club*. Tipping the scales at over 18 stone, he was to be crowned 'Mr Fit Club' by the end of the programme's run; he lost 24 per cent of his massive bulk.

Never married, Mick has been in three long-term relationships. He has a son, Michael (born in 1980), and twin daughters, Melissa and Natasha (born in 1987). Since 1994, Mick has been engaged to model Karen Davies.

On 14 May 2006, Mick was playing for Italy in the Celebrity World Cup Soccer Six tournament in Birmingham.

THE CAREER OF MICKY QUINN

Personal information

Youth clubs		
1979	Derby County	
Professional clubs*		
Years	**Club**	**Apps (goals)**
1979–81	Wigan Athletic	69 (19)
1982–83	Stockport County	63 (39)
1983–85	Oldham Athletic	80 (34)
1985–88	Pompey	121 (54)
1989–92	Newcastle United	115 (59)
1992–94	Coventry City	64 (25)
1994	Plymouth Argyle (loan)	3 (0)
1994	Watford (loan)	5 (0)

*Professional club appearances and goals counted for the League only

Pompey players born on 20 November

James (Jimmy) Henry Lawler b.1923;
Peter Joseph Mellor b.1925

Pompey player born on 21 November

Warren Anthony Neill b.1962

— MEMORABLE GAMES —

Ipswich Town v Pompey (Portman Road)
4 March 2000
Result: 0–1
Pompey goal scorer: Claridge

At the final whistle a chorus of boos rang round Portman Road after an Ipswich side chasing promotion to the Premiership slipped up at home to a lowly Pompey side, ending their 18-game unbeaten record.

Pompey managed to hold on after taking an early lead when Steve Claridge headed past Richard Wright from a Sammy Igoe delivery. This defeat did not prove costly for Ipswich as they gained promotion via the play-offs; however, it was the springboard for Pompey as they went on to win four of their next five games and eventually survive relegation finishing 18th, five points clear of the drop zone.

Pomp & Posterity – 1999–2000

After an awful start to the season, the club struggled but avoided relegation by five points.

Pompey players born on 22 November
Russell Hoult b.1972;
Guy Gavin Trise b.1933;
Ayegbeni Yakubu b.1982

— TO THE FRATTON FAITHFUL —

I was travelling back to Fareham from London Waterloo on Saturday, 25 March and had to change trains at Fratton. I was very concerned to see the platform absolutely packed with Portsmouth Football Club supporters and was quite nervous about getting on to the train with them. But I needn't have worried. Their behaviour was exemplary... They are a credit to you.

Letter to PFC from Mrs J M Breen in Pompey match programme, 19 August 2000

Pompey player born on 23 November
Anthony (Tony) Brian Fenton b.1979

— POMPEY XIs – ONE-HIT WONDERS —

These 11 players only managed one full League appearance for Pompey:

Name	Appearance
John Ashworth	vs Middlesbrough (18-05-1963)
Willie Bell	vs Leicester (04-02-1932)
Tommy Bernsten	vs Birmingham City (06-11-1999)
Ambrose Brown	vs West Brom (09-11-1935)
Bill Clarke	vs Wolverhampton W (08-12-1934)
Ian Collard	vs Carlisle (13-09-1975)
Jimmy Clugston	vs Luton Town (20-03-1957)
Liam Daish	vs Ipswich Town (07-02-1987)
Arthur Foxall	vs Hull City (24-01-1925)
Peter Higham	vs Birmingham City (25-02-1950)
Harold Moore	vs QPR (29-12-1923)

Pompey players born on 24 November
Eric Edward Duggins b.1931;
Gavin Terence Maguire b.1967;
Clive Robert Whitehead b.1955

— TO THE FRATTON FAITHFUL —

The New Millennium

Former Gillingham boss Tony Pulis arrived at Fratton Park as Alan Ball's successor. Players brought in by Pulis included winger Kevin Harper (football genius), Shaun Derry and keeper Russell Hoult. Pulis's reign was not a long one, and, on his departure, Steve Claridge came in as 'temporary player-manager'.

Although popular with the fans, Claridge's reign was to be short-lived and he was soon replaced by former Chelsea coach Graham Rix. Rix's time at Pompey proved to be ultimately unsuccessful.

Pompey player born on 25 November
Herbert Harold (Bert) Powell b.1880

Pompey players born on 26 November
Peter Russell Denyer b.1957;
David John Lee b.1969;
John Salvatore Ruggiero b.1954

Pomp & Posterity – 2001–02

Tragedy hit, as young goalkeeper Aaron Flahavan died in a car crash just a week before the start of the season.

With players like Crouch, Buxton, O'Neil and Zamperini and the skill of Prosinecki, things looked hopeful. However, results were inconsistent. Defeats to Leyton Orient and Colchester and a 5–0 thumping by WBA lead Mandaric to refuse to pay the players' wages. Redknapp sold top scorer Crouch for £5.5 million.

— TO THE FRATTON FAITHFUL —

Shaka got a better reception than me from the Reading fans!

Linvoy Primus after Reading away, 2002

Pompey players born on 27 November

Rodney (Rod) Charles Henwood b.1931;
Mark John Kelly b.1969;
Matthew Simon Taylor b.1981

— TRUE BLUE SONGS —

A popular chant from the 1950s:

1-2-3-4
Who do ya think we're shouting for?
P O M P E Y
Pompey!

2-4-6-8
Who do we appreciate?
P O M P E Y
Pompey.

And another from the 50s:

Hello, Hello, we are the Pompey boys,
Hello, Hello, we are the Pompey boys,
And if you are a Millwall fan
Climb back up your crane
We will follow the Pompey...

> **Pompey players born on 28 November**
> Michael (Mike) Roger Channon b.1948;
> Reginald (Reg) Flewin b.1920;
> Trevor John Senior b.1961

— TO THE FRATTON FAITHFUL —

Mandaric appointed former West Ham boss Harry Redknapp as Director of Football. When the axe finally fell on Rix, Redknapp was given the job as manager, assisted by former Pompey boss Jim Smith. Off the field, Peter Storrie had taken over as Chief Executive.

> **Pompey players born on 29 November**
> Kenneth (Kenny) George Black b.1963;
> Frank Haydock b.1940;
> Edward (Eddie) John Frank Howe b.1977;
> Septimus Eric (Sep) Rutherford b. 1907;
> Michael (Mike) Trebilcock b.1944

— 'ARRY, 'ARRY... 'ARRY, 'ARRY, 'ARRY... —

To say Harry Redknapp has been a significant figure at Pompey in the new millennium is perhaps something of an understatement. Harry joined Pompey as Director of Football at the end of the 2000/01 season, and was hailed by Milan Mandaric as one of his most important signings – perhaps even he did not realise how true this would turn out to be.

Prior to joining Pompey, Harry had started out his management career at Bournemouth, some 20 years previously. Working with a shoestring budget, he brought some of the most successful times the club had ever seen. Then, in 1992, he moved back to his native East End and became assistant manager to Billy Bonds at West Ham, before eventually replacing him as manager in August 1994.

The Hammers progressed steadily under Harry, playing attractive football and recording several top-half finishes in the Premiership, culminating in a fifth-place finish in the 1998/99 season and qualifying for Europe through the Intertoto Cup.

It was during his time at West Ham that Harry nurtured some of the most exciting young talent seen in England for some time, with the likes of Rio Ferdinand, Frank Lampard and Joe Cole coming through the ranks.

As time progressed, however, it became clear his relationship with West Ham

Chairman Terry Brown was becoming strained. Despite this, it still came as a shock when the Hammers announced they were parting company with Redknapp in May 2001.

And, so, Harry found himself at Fratton Park as Director of Football as the 2001/02 season began, with Graham Rix as manager. Never one to shy away from talking to the media, it became apparent throughout the season that Harry had itchy feet, and that perhaps it wasn't time for him to take the back seat just yet. This, coupled with indifferent form under Graham Rix, led to Harry's appointment as first-team manager in March 2002.

After an uneventful last two months of the 2001/02 season, thoughts turned to a summer rebuilding programme on the pitch. It was at this time that the ITV Digital television deal collapsed, leaving many First Division clubs short of much needed, and expected, revenue. Many clubs in the division had a quiet summer in the transfer market; however, recognising this as an opportunity, and possessing considerable personal wealth, Milan Mandaric authorised a spending spree (at least by the standards of the First Division at that time).

Harry's formula of bringing in top players towards the end of their career who still had plenty to offer came into its own now, with perhaps the most important signing of all being Paul Merson. Pompey blew the rest of the division away over the coming season, playing some of the best football seen at Fratton Park for a generation, and finishing the season as Champions.

Pompey went on to establish themselves in the Premiership, recording two home victories over Manchester United along the way.

Fans were then stunned when Harry was unveiled as manager of S***hampton one month later. The blow was somewhat softened by the 4–1 victory at Fratton Park in April 2005, and S***hampton's subsequent relegation from the Premiership.

Then, of course, the 'south-coast soap opera' took another remarkable twist. Harry was struggling to lift S***hampton in the Championship, and Pompey were going through a period of poor results under Alain Perrin, with the heart of the side Harry built destroyed following the sale of Steve Stone, Patrik Berger and Arjan De Zeeuw.

Against all the odds, Harry came back to Fratton Park almost exactly one year after he had walked out. Results didn't pick up immediately, but, with an injection of funds from new benefactor Sasha Gaydamak in the January transfer window, Harry turned the season around from almost certain relegation to surely one of the greatest escapes in the club's history.

One thing all fans will agree on is that Harry has done a remarkable job in turning the club around on the pitch, and has been one of the most successful managers ever at Pompey.

'ARRY SAID...

Merson is like a quarterback in American football. All you need are the receivers to get on the end of the passes.

Vincent Pericard is getting better with every game. But when I first bought him I thought I'd made a ricket.

We're a total footballing side. Andy Townsend has said all we can do is kick and chase. He must think I'm Harry Bassett from Wimbledon, not Harry Redknapp.

These fans are incredible – the best I've ever seen. They are fanatics and travel everywhere to watch us. It's their football club.

I wished I had backed us at 33–1 at the start of the season. I had a bet on Ipswich at 10–1 which shows how much of a judge I am!

If just spirit got you somewhere, then Havant and Waterlooville could be in the Premier League, but it doesn't work that way.

We're already 6–4 to be relegated from the Premiership. But we've got great support here and we'll give it a right go.

Why did I take the job? Because I was skint!

Brighton is like going to Sutton United in the FA Cup. Our fans were stuck up in the corner of the ground in the middle of nowhere.

We need another striker; we're struggling to put the ball in the net. I'm looking around for somebody for nothing who can get me 35 goals a season.

*I should never have been at S***hampton. I dived into it. I regretted it as soon as I got there.*

I think, deep down, most fans are glad to see me back. They know I'll only do my best.

*I knew when I came back from S***hampton I would never win over everybody, but I took Pompey into the Premiership and kept them there twice. People talk about great escapes but this has got to be one of the all-time great ones. I'm proud of what I've done here, I'm pleased for myself, as well as for the players and everyone at the club.*

THEY SAID ABOUT 'ARRY...

Harry's got a wealth of experience, and what he did last season was an absolute miracle. Players respect him; when he walks into the room, they know he's the boss. He's a wheeler and dealer too, that's a very strong part of his game

Tony Adams

So what next? Redknapp back at Pompey? In this barking mad part of the world, nothing is impossible.

***The Sun*, commenting on the goings on at Fratton pre-Harry's return**

Pompey players born on 30 November

Jamie Lawrence Ashdown b.1980;
George Gragam b.1944;
Andrew (Andy) Antonie McFarlane b.1966;
Jamie Ashdown b.1980

Pompey player born on 1 December

Malcolm Richardson Manley b.1949

Pompey player born on 2 December

David Stewart (Jock) McNab b.1897

— TO THE FRATTON FAITHFUL —

Pompey impressed me. Their fans came up in numbers and helped make it a good FA Cup atmosphere.

Alex Ferguson, 2003

Pompey players born on 3 December
Gordon Bartlett b.1955;
Paul Anthony Birch b.1968;
Stephen (Steve) Brian Foster b.1974;
Robert (Robbie) Shaun Taylor b.1967

— TRUE BLUE SONGS —

Super Steve's Blue and White Army
Super Steve's Blue and White Army.

Super Super Stevie
Super Super Stevie
Super Super Stevie
Super Stevie Claridge.

Saints are going down
Saints are going down
Super Pompey staying up
Super Pompey staying up.

My eyes are seeing the glory at the gates of Fratton Park
My eyes are seeing the glory at the gates of Fratton Park
My eyes are seeing the glory at the gates of Fratton Park
As the Blues go marching on on on
Glory glory Portsmouth city
Glory glory Portsmouth city
Glory glory Portsmouth city
As the Blues go marching on on on.

— MEMORABLE GAMES —

Walsall v Pompey (Bescot Stadium)
5 April 2003
Result: 1–2
Pompey goal scorers: Harper, Todorov

This game came towards the end of a very successful season, and, although some may find it a strange choice for a memorable game, for many, it was the moment Pompey fans finally believed they were going up.

A goal of sublime quality from Kevin Harper and an equally clinical header from Svetoslav Todorov looked to have settled the game after little more than half an hour, putting Pompey on course for their 25th victory of the League campaign.

But Hayden Foxe's careless mistake shortly before half-time gifted the hosts a goal their performance had barely deserved, and the League leaders were forced to endure a nervous second half at the Bescot Stadium.

The national media reported that Pompey's promotion to the Premiership was now a formality, and even the most pessimistic fans were starting to feel the same, although perhaps not admitting it for fear of tempting fate. However, the performance was not convincing, and, as such, the same articles were predicting a swift return to the Championship a year later.

Pompey's travelling faithful at the modest Bescot Stadium went home happy, and many will remember Paul Merson's premature celebrations when he thought he had scored near the final whistle – only for it to be cleared off the line at the last second!

Pompey players born on 4 December

Harry B Goodwin b.1903;
Edward (Ted) Hough b.1899;
Adam Lee Newton b.1980

— TO THE FRATTON FAITHFUL —

These Premiership virgins may have a look of Dad's Army, but they are beginning to worry established teams with their bullishness, organisation and lack of care for reputations.

***The Telegraph*, 2003**

Pompey players born on 5 December
Lee Roy Chapman b.1959;
Ian Michael Hendon b.1971;
Guy Wharton b.1916

— THE LEGEND THAT IS MERSE —

MERSON SAID...

When I signed and the gaffer said they'd finished in the bottom eight for the last few years, I thought, 'Oh no, what have I come for?'

On signing for Pompey 2002–03, the season the club won promotion

Even when I missed the penalty, the fans were still right behind us, and roaring us on. For them to sing my name after I missed the penalty was big stuff. They've been big all season.

In 2003

Becks sets a good example to kids – although I don't want my lads wearing sarongs when they get older!

Before a game with Manchester United

To be clapped off is something to be proud of. They don't clap too many here, do they?!

On the applause Millwall fans gave him after Pompey had beaten the Lions 5–0 there

I've never played on a pitch like that in all my career. We wouldn't have played on that at school.

Following a game against Leicester City in 2002

Our coach broke down and we had to come in cars. It was like The Italian Job. *I didn't know if I was going to rob a bank or play in a football match.*

After a match at Molineux in 2002

THEY SAID ABOUT MERSON...

Paul Merson will always be a big part of the history of this club. He gave 100 per cent for us and for that we thank him.

Milan Mandaric

Pompey players born on 6 December

Aaron Cook b.1979;
Shaun Peter Derry b.1977;
Clive Peter Green b.1959;
Stephen (Steve) William Henry Lovell b.1980;
Kevin John Russell b.1966

Pompey player born on 7 December

Edward Patrick (Teddy) McIntyre b.1881

Pompey player born on 8 December

Valery Mezague b.1983

Pompey players born on 9 December

William Cumming (Billy) Bell b.1906;
William (Bill) McCafferty b.1882

Pompey players born on 10 December

Lewis Edward Buxton b.1983;
Raymond (Ray) Christopher Daniel b.1964;
Sebastian Olszar b.1965;
Simon John Stapleton b.1968;
Archibald (Archie) Young b.1906

Pompey players born on 11 December

Christopher (Chris) Jason White b.1970;
Alexander (Alex) Glen b.1878

— MEMORABLE GAMES —

Pompey v Burnley (Fratton Park)
15 April 2003
Result: 1–0
Pompey goal scorer: Todorov

On 15 April 2003, Pompey finally reclaimed their place in English football's top flight after a 15-year absence. It was fitting that the feat was completed at Fratton Park.

Svetoslav Todorov grabbed the winner 17 minutes from time to become the club's first player since Guy Whittingham to score 20 goals in a season.

The goal finally arrived after Pompey – knocked off the top of the First Division by Leicester City on the previous Saturday for the first time since August 2002 – squandered numerous chances to go ahead. None more so than Paul Merson, who crashed his 12th-minute spot-kick against the crossbar after Gianluca Festa had been fouled in the area.

The final whistle began party scenes at Fratton Park as Pompey ended their 15-year wait and at the same time moved two points clear of Leicester – with both teams having four games remaining – the focus now was firmly on the race for the title.

Pompey player born on 12 December
Daniel (Danny) Martin Hinshelwood b.1975

— TO THE FRATTON FAITHFUL —

Someone suggested to me we should retire his shirt for next season and I agreed straight away. No one else will wear it, even if we make a new signing.

Graham Rix, after the Aaron Flahavan tragedy

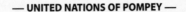

— UNITED NATIONS OF POMPEY —

Sven Andreasson, Striker, Born: Hadsel, Norway (1998/99)
John Aloisi, Striker, Born: Adelaide, Australia (1997–99)
Noel Blake, Defender, Born: Kingston, Jamaica (1984–88)
Tommy Christensen, Striker, Born: Denmark (1985/86)
Mathias Svensson, Striker, Born: Boras Sweden (1996–98)
Marcel Gaillard, Midfield, Born: Chaleris, Belgium (1950–53)
Marc Keller, Midfield, Born: Colmar, France (2000/01)
John Kerr, Striker, Born: Toronto, Canada (1987/88)
Bjorn (Benny) Kristensen, Midfield, Born: Malling, Denmark (1992–95)
Nikos Kyzerides, Striker, Born: Salonika, Greece (1998–99)
Harry Lunn, Winger, Born: Lurgan, Northern Ireland (1947/48)
Scott McGarvey, Striker, Born: Glasgow, Scotland (1984–86)
Tony Macken, Midfield, Born: Waterford, Republic of Ireland (1975/76)
Stefani Miglioranzi, Midfield, Born: Pocos de Caldas, Brazil (1998–2001)
Jeff Peron, Midfield, Born: St Omer, France (1998–2000)
Reg Pickett, Striker, Born: Bareilly, India (1949–57)
Mart Poom, Goalkeeper, Born: Tallin, Estonia (1994–96)
Predrag Radosavljevic (Preki), Winger, Born: Belgrade, Yugoslavia (1994/95)
Jason Rees, Midfield, Born: Pontypridd, Wales (1994–97)
Mladen Rudonja, Midfield, Born: Slovenia (2001/01)
Roy Smith, Inside Left, Born: Rawalpindi, India (1961–63)
Michalis Vlachos, Midfield, Born: Athens, Greece (1997–2000)

Pompey players born on 13 December

David (Dave) Griffiths b.1937;
Lionel Arthur Raymond Phillips b.1929

— GUY WHITTINGHAM'S DREAM TEAM XI —

Alan Knight

Warren Neil   Kit Symons   Andy Awford   John Beresford

Steve Wigley   Darren Anderton   Kevin Ball   Mark Chamberlain

Paul Walsh   Steve Claridge

Subs: Aaron Flahavan, Ray Daniel, Martin Kuhl, Jeff Peron

Pompey players born on 14 December

Ronald (Ron) Humpston b.1923;
Andrew (Andy) Nicholas Rollings b.1954

Pompey players born on 15 December

Aaron Adam Flahavan b.1975;
Robert (Bobby) Gordon John Smith b.1941

— TRUE BLUE FACT —

Until recently, TV presenter Fred Dinenage was a Director at Pompey.

Pompey players born on 16 December

Mark Anthony Blacke b.1970

Pomp & Posterity – 2002–03

The collapse of ITV Digital meant most First Division clubs became subdued financially but Mandaric, on the back of the sale of Crouch, gave Harry Redknapp the green light to go on a transfer spending spree.

The arrival of Steve Stone brought valuable experience to the side along with the likes of striker Svetoslav Todorov, Shaka Hislop, Arjan De Zeeuw, Matthew Taylor and Vincent Pericard.

The signing of former England midfielder Paul Merson to Fratton Park helped Pompey achieve their best start to a season since the late 1940s. January saw the arrival of Yakubu Aiyegbeni from Maccabi Haifa who was to become instrumental in Pompey sitting at the top of the table for most of that season.

Pompey won the Championship and promotion.

Svetoslav Todorov took the player of the season award.

Pompey player born on 17 December

Courtney Leon Pitt b.1981

2002–03 League Division One

		P	W	D	L	F	A	W	D	L	F	A	Pts
1	**Pompey**	**46**	**17**	**3**	**3**	**52**	**22**	**12**	**8**	**3**	**45**	**23**	**98**
2	Leicester City	46	16	5	2	40	12	10	9	4	33	28	92
3	Sheffield Utd	46	13	7	3	38	23	10	4	9	34	29	80
4	Reading	46	13	3	7	33	21	12	1	10	28	25	79
5	Wolverhampton W	46	9	10	4	40	19	11	6	6	41	25	76
6	Nottingham Forest	46	14	7	2	57	23	6	7	10	25	27	74
7	Ipswich	46	10	5	8	49	39	9	8	6	31	25	70
8	Norwich	46	14	4	5	36	17	5	8	10	24	32	69
9	Millwall	46	11	6	6	34	32	8	3	12	25	37	66
10	Wimbledon	46	12	5	6	39	28	6	6	11	37	45	65
11	Gillingham	46	10	6	7	33	31	6	8	9	23	34	62
12	Preston NE	46	11	7	5	44	29	5	6	12	24	41	61
13	Watford	46	11	5	7	33	26	6	4	13	21	44	60
14	Crystal Palace	46	8	10	5	29	17	6	7	10	30	35	59
15	Rotherham	46	8	9	6	27	25	7	5	11	35	37	59
16	Burnley	46	10	4	9	35	44	5	6	12	30	45	55
17	Walsall	46	10	3	10	34	34	5	6	12	23	35	54
18	Derby County	46	9	5	9	33	32	6	2	15	22	42	52
19	Bradford City	46	7	8	8	27	35	7	2	14	24	38	52
20	Coventry City	46	6	6	11	23	31	6	8	9	23	31	50
21	Stoke City	46	9	6	8	25	25	3	8	12	20	44	50
22	Sheffield Wed	46	7	7	9	29	32	3	9	11	27	41	46
23	Brighton	46	7	6	10	29	31	4	6	13	20	36	45
24	Grimsby Town	46	5	6	12	26	39	4	6	13	22	46	39

Pompey players born on 18 December

Thomas (Tommy) Bernsten b.1973;
Kevin Paul Dillon b.1959;
Justin Charles Edinburgh b.1969

Pompey players born on 19 December

Peter Philip Harris b.1925;
David Hillier b.1969

Pomp & Posterity – 18 September 2003

Pompey Chairman Milan Mandaric received the ultimate tribute when made an honorary Freeman of the City of Portsmouth.

Pompey player born on 20 December
Terence (Terry) James Parker b.1983

— TRUE BLUE FACT —

Pompey defender Dave Waterman was born in Guernsey.

Pompey players born on 21 December
James (Jimmy) Emslie Irvine Bannerman Dawson b.1927;
Robert Ainsley Wolleaston b.1979

— TO THE FRATTON FAITHFUL —

Paul and Teddy

Paul Merson left Pompey a hero having done the job and, with doubts over whether he was up to Premiership football, joined Walsall. In came Teddy Sheringham and Patrik Berger to assist the squad in the huge step up to Premiership football.

Pomp & Posterity - 2003–04

The south-coast party continued on the first game of the season when an early kick-off and a 2–1 home win against Aston Villa saw Pompey top the Premiership - if only for less than three hours! A great start put Pompey at the top of the table after three games.

In that first season in the top flight, Pompey had a good home record but were let down by a poor away one. By autumn, Pompey were fairly safe mid-table after impressive results like a 1–1 draw at Highbury against Arsenal and a 1–0 home win against Liverpool. After a fraught mid-season plagued with injuries, Redknapp was (not for the first time) 'down to the bare bones'. By March, relegation looked a real possibility. To add to this, they had been beaten twice at St Mary's, once in the League and once in the Cup. The season ended with the club finishing a creditable 13th place and rumours of a rift between the Chair and the manager, after speculation about the future of 19-goal Yakubu.

— SEASON 2002–03 LEAGUE DIVISION 1 —

Date		Team	Result	Gate
10 Aug	H	Nottm For	W 2–0	18910
13 Aug	A	Sheffield Utd	D 1–1	16093
17 Aug	A	C Palace	W 3–2	18315
24 Aug	H	Watford	W 3–0	17901
26 Aug	A	Grimsby	W 1–0	5770
31 Aug	H	Brighton	W 4–2	19031
07 Sept	A	Gillingham	W 3–1	8717
14 Sept	H	Millwall	W 1–0	17201
17 Sept	H	Wimbledon	W 4–1	18837
21 Sept	A	Norwich	L 0–1	21335
28 Sept	H	Bradford City	W 3–0	18459
05 Oct	A	Rotherham	W 3–2	8604
19 Oct	H	Coventry	D 1–1	18837
26 Oct	A	Burnley	W 3–0	15788
29 Oct	H	Preston NE	W 3–2	18637
02 Nov	H	Leicester	L 0–2	19107
06 Nov	A	Wolves	D 1–1	27022
09 Nov	A	Derby	W 2–1	26587
16 Nov	H	Stoke	W 3–0	18701
23 Nov	A	Sheffield Wed	W 3–1	16602
30 Nov	H	Walsall	W 3–2	17701
07 Dec	A	Reading	D 0–0	23462
14 Dec	A	Stoke	D 1–1	13330
21 Dec	H	Ipswich	D 1–1	19130
26 Dec	H	C Palace	D 1–1	19217
28 Dec	A	Nottm For	W 2–1	28165
01 Jan	A	Watford	D 2–2	15048
13 Jan	H	Sheffield Utd	L 1–2	18872
18 Jan	A	Brighton	D 1–1	6848
01 Feb	H	Grimsby Town	W 3–0	19428
08 Feb	H	Derby County	W 6–2	19503
17 Feb	A	Leicester City	D 1–1	31775
22 Feb	H	Gillingham	W 1–0	19521
01 Mar	A	Millwall	W 5–0	9697
04 Mar	A	Wimbledon	L 1–2	10356
12 Mar	H	Norwich City	W 3–2	19221

15 Mar	H	Wolves	W 1–0	19558
19 Mar	A	Coventry City	W 4–0	13922
22 Mar	A	Preston NE	D 1–1	16665
05 Apr	A	Walsall	W 2–1	7899
12 Apr	H	Sheffield Wed	L 1–2	19524
15 Apr	H	Burnley	W 1–0	19221
18 Apr	A	Ipswich Town	L 0–3	29396
21 Apr	H	Reading	W 3–0	19535
27 Apr	H	Rotherham	W 3–2	19420
04 May	A	Bradford City	W 5–0	19088

P42 W25 D11 L6 F99 A45 Pts86
League Position 1st (Promoted as Champions)

Appearances: S Hislop, P Merson, S Todorov, N Quashie, A De Zeeuw, M Taylor, L Primus, G Festa, K Harper, V Pericard, S Stone, T Sherwood, L Diabate, A Yakubu, D Burton, C Robinson, G O'Neil, P Ritchie, J Crowe, M Burchill, R Hughes, H Foxe, E Tavlaridis, L Bradbury, C Tiler, M Heikkinen, E Howe, L Buxton, Y Kawaguchi

Pompey players born on 22 December
Ernest (Ernie) Gadsden b.1895;
Paul Stephen Musselwhite b.1968;
Luke Raymond Nightingale b.1980;
Jason Mark Rees b.1969

— TO THE FRATTON FAITHFUL —

At one point I travelled on five flights, via seven airports in just two days, with meetings in between as well, so it was pretty tiring.

Peter Storrie on transfer dealings

Pompey player born on 23 December
Matthew (Matt) Richard Robinson b.1974

— CELEBRITY SUPPORTERS —

Brian Howe

Brian Howe was the lead singer of rock group Bad Company throughout the 1980s and early 90s, selling millions of records – he is also a big Pompey fan.

Despite living in America, Brian still keeps tabs on Pompey, and became well known to Pompey fans when he attempted to buy the club with American businessman Vince Wolanin in 1999. The club was in administration at the time, and several parties bid for the club. For a long time, it seemed that Howe and Wolanin were in pole position to purchase the club; however, in the end, Milan Mandaric took control.

Brian's love for football has seen him become heavily involved in the sport on the other side of the Atlantic. He is involved with The Revolution with ex-Pompey player Paul Mariner and former Liverpool player Steve Nichol.

Fred Dinenage

> *A few years ago I was walking with our chairman, Milan Mandaric, around the pitch side to our seats for a game at Preston. He, like me, was very impressed that a Preston supporter seemed desperate to get my autograph. After I had signed, the supporter asked me what it said.*
>
> *'Fred Dinenage,' I replied.*
>
> *'Oh,' said the disappointed fan, 'I thought you were Fred Dibnah!'*
>
> **Fred Dinenage**

It is well known that Fred is a Pompey fan, as he never shies away from stating his allegiance. He is best known in the area for presenting the news on *Meridian Tonight* for ITV Meridian – considered by many fans to be biased in its presentation and coverage towards the western end of the M27. Fred provides a much needed 'Pompey perspective' to the local media and has earned the respect of fans in the blue end of Hampshire.

Nationally, Fred is better known for appearing in television programmes such as *Gambit*, *Tell The Truth* and *How 2*. He is perhaps less well known for his writing, including his ghosting of an autobiography of the Kray twins.

His passion for Pompey saw him installed as a Board Member under the Chairmanship of Milan Mandaric; however, Fred stepped down from this role at the end of the 2005/06 season. Despite this, he is still a regular at Fratton Park.

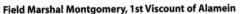

Field Marshal Montgomery, 1st Viscount of Alamein

> *I send my very hearty congratulations to the manager and all the team for the splendid way in which they have come on at the end of the season and again won the First Division Championship. I somehow knew we would do it.*
>
> **Telegram from Field Marshal Viscount Montgomery (Club President)**

Field Marshal Montgomery was President of Portsmouth Football Club during the back-to-back Championship-winning years of 1949 and 1950. He took a great interest in the club and was one of the first to express his delight at winning the Championships.

Originally from London, 'Monty' commanded allied forces at the battle of El Alamein, which was a major turning point in the Second World War. His troops were largely responsible for the expulsion of Axis forces from North Africa. He was later a prominent Commander in Italy and North-West Europe, where he was in command of all Allied ground forces during Operation Overlord and then until after the Battle of Normandy.

One of the heroes of the Second World War, Monty is surely the most famous person ever to be associated with Pompey. Monty died at his home in Alton in 1976 at the age of 88.

Anthony Minghella

Anthony Minghella is an Academy Award-winning film director, playwright and screenwriter – and a big Pompey fan as well.

Anthony won an Oscar for his directing of *The English Patient* in 1996. This is when his name really hit the headlines; however, he had been involved in television for several years, editing and working on scripts for shows such as *Grange Hill* and *Inspector Morse*. He subsequently moved into films and has worked on films such as *Cold Mountain*, *The Talented Mr Ripley* and *Play*.

He is the chairman of the British Film Institute and has recently extended his talents to working in opera.

As well as living the high life and rubbing shoulders with some of Hollywood's finest, Anthony can also be found sitting in the South Stand upper on a match day at Fratton Park!

Pompey players born on 24 December

Sydney (Syd) James Asher b.1930;
Neil William Barrett b.1981;
Kenneth Dennis Hall b.1930

Pomp & Posterity – 2004–05

Summer signings included Jamie Ashdown, Ricardo Fuller and David Unsworth and the club made a good start. In October, Pompey were unbeaten, and defeats had been inflicted on Manchester United and Spurs. Redknapp won manager of the month. However, following three successive defeats, Harry and Jim resigned on 23 November 2004, with Redknapp declaring that he needed a break from football.

Pompey fans were left stunned when a fortnight later Redknapp was announced as new manager of rivals S***hampton. He had assured Pompey fans the day he left Fratton that he would never 'go down the road'. He took Jim Smith and Kevin Bond with him.

Zajec took temporary control at Pompey and he started well, with away victories at Bolton and Palace, together with draws at Newcastle and Liverpool. But perhaps the most memorable game of that period was a 3–2 win over WBA – Pompey had been 2–1 down with 10 minutes to play. But in the second half of the season the club went more than three months without a win. This run included a 2–1 defeat to S***hampton in the FA Cup after a very doubtful penalty awarded late in the game. Eventually, caretaker Zajec was moved back to his original job as Director of Football and Alain Perrin was installed as manager in April 2005.

Despite having dropped from ninth on Boxing Day to 17th by April, Perrin turned things round. Probably the highlight of the season was when Redknapp brought his new team to Fratton. Harry could only look on as Pompey cruised to a 4–1 victory with a fantastic display, including two goals from Lua Lua who left the pitch injured.

This victory proved to be quite a nail in S***hampton's coffin. They lost to Manchester United in a dramatic last game of the season as Pompey were beaten at the Hawthorns. This meant the Baggies stayed up and S***hampton were relegated from the top flight. Pompey fans celebrated finally becoming the top dogs of the south coast and the fact that justice was done on the last day of the season.

Pompey player born on 25 December
Christopher (Chris) Kamara b.1957

— TRUE BLUE FACTS —

When Alan Knight played at Norwich on 3 January 2000, one of his teammates was Jason Crowe who hadn't been born when Alan made his debut in April 1978.

Pompey's George Charles Hunter was born in 1896 in Peshawar, India. He played three times for the Football League.

Pompey players born on 26 December
John William (Billy) Hindmarsh 1919;
James Duncan Keene b.1985;
Alexsander Rodic b.1979

— TO THE FRATTON FAITHFUL —

It has apparently been thus for 250 years

The necessity of living in the midst of the diabolical citizens of Portsmouth is a real and unavoidable calamity. It is a doubt to me if there is such another collection of demons upon the whole earth.

General James Wolfe, 1758

Pompey players born on 27 December
Robert (Bobby) Doyle b. 1953; Ralph Vincent Holten b.1896;
Mark Nicholas Stimson b.1967; Derek Keith Weddle b.1935

— TRUE BLUE FACT —

Pompey's list of players who have made over 300 League appearances includes three goalkeepers – Alan Knight (683), John Milkins (344) and Jock Gilfillan (330).

Pompey players born on 28 December
Andrew (Andy) Perry b.1962;
Lumana Tresor Lua Lua b.1980

— TO THE FRATTON FAITHFUL —

Find out who that trumpet-playing Louis Armstrong is among your supporters and tell him to stick the instrument where the sun doesn't shine. He sounds like someone who has had about 17 pints of lager before the game got started – no wonder they lost.

Richie Woodhall, former WBC Super-Middleweight Boxing Champion and West Brom fan

— MEMORABLE GAMES —

Pompey v S*hampton (Fratton Park)**
24 April 2005
Thrashing: 4–1
Pompey goal scorers: Yakubu, De Zeeuw, Lua Lua (2)

Although this one is still fresh in many people's minds, it will surely be remembered for many years to come.

This game had everything, and was immensely satisfying for all Pompey supporters. In this one game, the Blues guaranteed their first League finish above S***hampton since 1960, they left S***hampton stranded at the bottom of the Premiership facing almost certain relegation, and, of course, they put one over the manager, Harry Redknapp, that had 'gone down the road' earlier in the season.

The atmosphere was electric and the players responded accordingly. Every 50/50 ball was contested and not one bottled by a Pompey player.

Within four minutes, Lua Lua was brought down by Niemi for a penalty. Then, shortly after, on 17 minutes, captain Arjan De Zeeuw headed in a Patrik Berger free-kick.

Henri Camara thought he had got S***hampton going with a solo effort on 20 minutes. But then Lua Lua, a man on fire, struck two in five minutes as S***hampton's defence fell apart.

With 26 minutes gone, and 4–1 to Pompey the score, Fratton Park didn't know how to react with some stunned into silence, while others sang. The singing soon took over, however, as the game petered out, the result already a foregone conclusion.

Nearing the final whistle, all that could be heard were the Pompey fans taunting their rivals (those who were brave enough to stay). Although relegation was not yet mathematically confirmed for S***hampton, this was clearly the result that knocked the stuffing out of them, and led to their relegation a couple of weeks later.

2004–05 Premiership Table

		P	W	D	L	F	A	W	D	L	F	A	Pts
1	Chelsea	38	14	5	0	35	6	15	3	1	37	9	95
2	Arsenal	38	13	5	1	54	19	12	3	4	33	17	83
3	Man Utd	38	12	6	1	31	12	10	5	4	27	14	77
4	Everton	38	12	2	5	24	15	6	5	8	21	31	61
5	Liverpool	38	12	4	3	31	15	5	3	11	21	26	58
6	Bolton	38	9	5	5	25	18	7	5	7	24	26	58
7	Middlesbrough	38	9	6	4	29	19	5	7	7	24	27	55
8	Man City	38	8	6	5	24	14	5	7	7	23	25	52
9	Tottenham	38	9	5	5	36	22	5	5	9	11	19	52
10	Aston Villa	38	8	6	5	26	17	4	5	10	19	35	47
11	Charlton	38	8	4	7	29	29	4	6	9	13	29	46
12	Birmingham	38	8	6	5	24	15	3	6	10	16	31	45
13	Fulham	38	8	4	7	29	26	4	4	11	23	34	44
14	Newcastle	38	7	7	5	25	25	3	7	9	22	32	44
15	Blackburn	38	5	8	6	21	22	4	7	8	11	21	42
16	**Pompey**	**38**	**8**	**4**	**7**	**30**	**26**	**2**	**5**	**12**	**13**	**33**	**39**
17	West Brom	38	5	8	6	17	24	1	8	10	19	37	34
18	Crystal Palace	38	6	5	8	21	19	1	7	11	20	43	33
19	Norwich	38	7	5	7	29	32	0	7	12	13	45	33
20	S***hampton	38	5	9	5	30	30	1	5	13	15	36	32

Pompey player born on 29 December

Johnson William (Willie) Haywood b.1920

Pompey player born on 30 December

William (Billy) Henry Rafferty b.1950

Pomp & Posterity – 2005–06

This season was to be one of the toughest for Pompey with the management crisis continuing in the most unexpected way.

Lauren Robert arrived from Newcastle while Yakubu left for Middlesbrough and no new contracts were offered to Stone or Berger. Popular De Zeeuw left to join Premiership new boys Wigan Athletic. A string of bad results saw pressure pile up for Perrin and he left Pompey in December 2005. This paved the way for the final twist in the south-coast management saga when Redknapp, having left S***hampton, apologising for his deflection, returned to Fratton Park. His first job was to save Pompey from relegation.

January 2006 saw Mandaric sell a stake in the club to businessman Alexandre Gaydamak. This enabled Redknapp to do 'some shopping' in the January transfer window to strengthen the side and try to avoid the drop. The new additions included Pedro Mendes, Sean Davies, Noe Paramot from Spurs and the loan of Andres D'Alessandro from Vfl Wolfsburg. After a win at home against Manchester City, Pompey found the form needed to escape relegation and this was confirmed with a win at Wigan Athletic which secured safety and prompted a Pompey party at the JJB Stadium!

In 2006, Pompey goalkeeping legend Alan Knight who left the club in the summer of 2005 left England to pursue a career with American Major Soccer League side FC Dallas.

— TRUE BLUE SONGS —

Harry and Jim,
Harry and Jim,
Harry and Jim...

Eagle... Eagle... Eagle...

Harry Redknapp's Blue and White Army,
Harry Redknapp's Blue and White Army!

— TRUE BLUE FACT —

Pompey's highest ever home attendance was 51,385 against Derby County in the FA Cup 6th round on 26 February 1949.

Pompey players born on 31 December
Thomas (Tommy) Hird b.1912; Robert (Bobby) McAlinden b.1917

— TO THE FRATTON FAITHFUL —

Lucky to be a true blue...!

While travelling in the Yemeni mountains near Taiz, after stopping at a roadblock, Tony Restall escaped being murdered by Muslim fanatics because they thought his Pompey sticker was an Islamic emblem.

Tony, 56, was ambushed by bandits armed with AK-47 rifles. They dragged him and his armed guard from their car.

But when the assailants noticed Tony's club sticker with its moon and star symbols, signifiers of the Islamic faith, in a window of his car, they took it that he was a practising Muslim.

Restall, a businessman and a Portsmouth-born Pompey fan, was working as a European Union adviser helping the Yemeni government set up a free-trade zone in Aden. After the incident, he said, 'The tribesmen descended upon me like a pack of wolves. They had bloodshot eyes and I was terrified they would kill me.

'I was able to convince them that, although I was Western, I was helping Muslims in the area.

'In my limited Arabic, I understood that they wanted to use me as a hostage to extract money from the EU and if I refused would kill me. They marched me around to the back of the vehicle and then stopped as they noticed the two stickers on the screen – an EU motif and a Pompey supporters' club badge.

'Immediately they started pointing at the PFC logo and I explained I was a follower of Islam who was specifically helping Muslims in Yemen.

'There was much shouting and gesturing and then, as if by magic, we were bundled into the vehicle and told to drive away quickly.

'Thank God they didn't read English!'

— TO THE FRATTON FAITHFUL —

I have no intention of getting out, so they are wasting their time, but they should be aware that, if I were to go, then the club would go with me.

Under-fire club chairman John Deacon

— MILAN THE MAN —

Milan Mandaric came to Pompey when the future of the club was in serious doubt. Born in the former Yugoslavia and raised in Serbia, Milan was involved in his father's machine shop and developed it into the largest business in the country.

He later moved to the United States and went on to form his own company manufacturing computer components.

Having always had a passion for football (he had played as a young man in Serbia), he became actively involved in two clubs in the US; however, unsure of the popularity of soccer in America, he turned to Europe.

Then, in the summer of 1999, after being introduced by former Pompey player Preki, Mandaric took over Portsmouth Football Club. Milan brought not only vital investment to the club but also an obvious passion for its future success and has played a massive part in 'waking the sleeping giant' of the south coast. His time at Pompey will be remembered for some of the club's best achievements and his legacy will never be forgotten. In the words of the Fratton Faithful, there truly is 'only one Milan'.

MILAN SAID...

Chairmen like to think we are all shrewd businessmen but we are kidding ourselves. We are just fans.

Milan the fan

From the manager to the janitor who sweeps the floor, we want to be the best.

After buying Portsmouth FC

I'm paying for players that I never saw play for Pompey and that irritates the hell out of me.

Revealing the club had finally paid for striker John Aloisi in August 1997

It's a dream. When we wake up to the reality, we will roll up our sleeves and work hard to stay in the Premiership.

There is hope and these are the faces I have seen again and again, year after year, mostly etched in misery.

In 2003

When you are in the trenches, you know who your friends are.

The fans are my friends and you don't desert a friend when he is in need, do you? If I leave this club, it will be when they are at the top.

I asked George Best, 'Do the supporters sing the Chairman's name at matches?' He said, 'Yes, of course they do, Milan, but they use different words.'

In every boardroom we visit in every part of the country, chairmen and directors talk to us with envy about the level and volume of our support away from home

Acknowledging the fans' support for him

I have been involved in football for many years but this is some of the greatest support I've ever seen.

On what attracted him to Pompey

We managed to survive relegation. But I've got to confess, I went through hell in those matches towards the end of the season.

On surviving relegation

He will wear the No. 8 shirt. We've been saving that for him.

On signing Robert Prosinecki

I've always said Pompey are the biggest club in Hampshire, but it's a great feeling now we're officially kings of the mountain.

On S*hampton's relegation**

We are truly champions – and the city of Portsmouth is a champion city.

On victory parade day, 2003

The plans for the new stadium and Pompey Village are progressing quite positively... This plan goes on and goes forward, no matter what happens on the pitch.

On the new ground... the search goes on

I've virtually paid all of those off with the exception of Foster. Foster was one of a string of 'Aussies' signed by Venables which included Robbie Enes and Hamilton Thorp, who cost £250,000 and made just one appearance each before returning down under. Venables's only 'Aussie' success was John Aloisi.

On Venables's Aussie purchases

I returned to the USA to attend a high-profile business function. With it being known that I am a regular traveller, both across North America and across the Atlantic, I was asked, 'Where do you feel the safest?' My answer was: 'In the KJC Stand.'

Post 9/11

This guy's made of rubber.

On Yoshi Kawaguchi

THEY SAID ABOUT MILAN...

— TRUE BLUE SONGS —

Milan, there's only one Milan,
There's only one Milan!

Anyone who walks into a pub and immediately puts £300 behind the bar to buy free drinks for all is obviously going to be welcomed back any time they like.

Fan on Milan meeting fans at local pub

Milan is a visionary. He simply doesn't contemplate failure and is certain of success.

Former Pompey Director Fred Dinenage

Milan's not a 'flash Harry', he's a normal guy who has worked hard and earned his money. He loves football. He has pumped a lot of money into the club and the people here appreciate it. You have only got to sit in the ground to hear what the fans think of him. He is just a very special man and he deserves everything he gets. I always say that the good guys win and he is a good guy, and as a friend he is special to me.

George Best, 2004

POMPEY PUB

The Good Companion
Eastern Road, Milton

FAMOUS PRE-WAR PLAYERS WHOSE BIRTHDAYS CAN'T BE TRACED

Messina Wilson (Dick) Allman b.1883

John Robert (Jack) Bainbridge b.1880

William J. Blyth b.1885

Robert (Bob) Blyth b.1870

Arthur Brown b.1900

John B Brown b.1895

Arthur Chadwick b.1875

Thomas (Tom) Cleghorn b.1871

Henry Croft b.1900

Frank Donoghue b.1916

A L Duncan b.1891

John (Jack) Fletcher b.1910

D G Gair b.1880

William Goss b.1879

James A Hogg b.1892

Thomas (Tom) McDonald b.1887

Thomas McKenzie b.1880

Thomas (Tom) Newton b.1890

William O'Hare b.1910

Thomas Herbert (Bert) Pearce b.1889

Ronald (Ronnie) Ranson b.1920

James Reid b.1890

John William Robinson b.1900

Frank Rollinson b.1885

Thomas (Tommy) Rowe b.1913

John Shankly b.1900

Frederick Elliot Shaw b.1891

Thomas Shipley b.1905

John William (Jack) Smelt b.1895

John (Jack) Smith b.1885

William (Billy) Smith b.1872

Thomas Worsley (Tommy) Stewart b.1881

James Frank (Frank) Stringfellow b.1890

Robert (Bob) Struthers b.1879

Eden Taylor b.1916

John Harold (Harry) Taylor b.1888

Emil Guy (Ernie) Thompson b.1892

Edward E (Old Hookey) Turner b.1877

Harold (Harry) Turner b.1877
Joseph (Joe) Turner b.1894
Richard William (Billy) Turner b.1884
Alexander C (Sandy) Wardrope b.1886
John (Jack) Warner b.1883
James (Dougal) Watson b.1883
Edward C (Jesse) Weeks b.1908
Roderick Ernest (Rod) Welsh b.1912
Thomas (Tom) Wilkie b.1876
Ernest W Williams b.1880
David Wilson b.1883
John Robert (Jock) Wilson b.1900
William (Bill) Wilson b.1902
Horace Duncan Wright b.1892
William Yates b.1883
George Young b.1880

— POMPEY HAMMERS POST-WAR XI —

Pompey players who have also appeared in the claret and blue of East London

Jim Standen
Sebastien Schemmel
Hayden Foxe
Martin Allen
Teddy Sheringham
John Moncur
Glen Johnson
Alan Stephenson
Marc Keller
Eyal Berkovic
Svetoslav Todorov

Subs (slightly heavy on the keepers)

Pavel Srnicek
David James
David Unsworth
Adam Newton
Ernie Tindall
Shaka Hislop
Sasa Ilic
Adrian Whitbread
Lee Chapman

— POMPEY'S PRE-WAR HAMMERS 5-A-SIDE TEAM —

Alex Kane
Alex McDonald
Bill 'Sunny' Jim Kirby
Steve Smith
Billy James

— TRUE BLUE SONGS —

'Arry, 'Arry, give us a wave,
'Arry, give us a wave!

Shall we sing a song for you!
Shall we sing a song for you!

Blue Army, Blue Army, Blue Army!

— ANOTHER POEM BY BOB —

The Final Chapter

He came to us some years ago, with Pompey on her knees.
He bought the club, he paid the debts, and did his best to please.
He picked us up, he'd dust us down, and made a brand new start,
We knew the blood of PFC was there inside his heart.
This man possessed such passion, he strived for folk like me,
With problems mounting, overcame, endurance was the key.
So many disappointing times, tough choices to be made,
But in his head, and in his heart, he knew we'd make the grade.
Sometimes the faithful worried, at home or in the pub,
Our history shows he'd always act, for Portsmouth Football Club.
At last we turned the corner, with Pompey riding high.
Our club was taken seriously, and reaching for the sky.
A club with strong foundations, and building day by day,
Our team could mix it with the best, the Milan Mandaric way.
The freedom of our city, an honour he deserves.
So richly earned with spine and steel, and rarely signs of nerves.
Alas he feels it's time to go, and most will shed a tear.
But even there he's done us proud, we've nothing now to fear.
As for myself I know I'm sad, and all that's left to say,
'Because of him, our club survived, is where it is today.'
I know I speak for all in blue, for each and every fan,
We're really proud to sing that chant, 'There's only one Milan'.

LONG LIVE MILAN MANDARIC

— POMPEY SUPPORTERS CLUBS —

Pompey Central Branch Supporters Club: www.pompeyfan.com
Pompey Independent Supporters
Chichester Supporters Club
Isle of Wight Supporters Club: www.iwpsc.co.uk
London Supporters Club
South West Supporters: www.pfcswsc.co.uk
South Wales Supporters: http://uk.geocities.com/swapsonline
Midlands Supporters Club
Northern Blues
Pompey Scottish Supporters: http://members.lycos.co.uk/clanpompey
Irish Blue Army Supporters Club
Pompey Anorak Brigade: www.pompey.org
American Supporters Club: www.pfcusa.net
Australian Supporters Club: www.pompeydownunder.net
Dubai Pompey Supporters Club
Senegal (W Africa) Supporters Club
Costa Del Sol Pompey Supporters Club
Pompey Army Belguim

— BIBLIOGRAPHY —

Selected biographies:

Smith, J, with Cass, B, (2000) *Jim Smith: The Autobiography – It's Only A Game*, London: Andre Deutsch Ltd
Knight, A, with Jeffs, P, and Farmery, C (2003) *Legend*, Legendary Publishing

Reference works:

Belton, B (1997) *Bubbles, Hammers and Dreams*, Derby: Breedon Books
Belton, B (1998) *The First and Last Englishmen*, Derby: Breedon Books
Belton, B (1999) *Days of Iron*, Derby: Breedon Books
Belton, B (2003) *Founded on Iron*, Gloucestershire: Tempus
Belton, B (2006) *The Lads of '23*, Nottingham: Tony Brown
Belton, B (2006) *The Men of '64*, Gloucestershire: Tempus
Butler, B (1987) *The Football League 1888-1988: The Official Illustrated History*, London: Queen Anne Press
Cook, C, and Stevenson, J (1988) *Modern British History*, London: Longman
Fabian, A H, and Green, G (eds.) (1961) *Associated Football*, London: Caxton
Farmery C, (2005) *Portsmouth: The Modern Era – A Complete Record*, Essex: Desert Island Books Limited

Farror, M, and Lamming, D (1972) *A Century of English International Football 1872–1972*, London: Hale

Gibson, A, and Pickford, W (1905) *Association Football and the Men Who Have Made It*, London

Green, G (1953) *The History of the Football Association*, London: The Naldrett Press

Harding, J (1991) *For the Good of the Game: The Official History of the Professional Footballers' Association*, London: Robson

Holmes, R (2001) *Pompey Players 1920–2001: The Official Guide to All Portsmouth's Football League Players*, Portsmouth: Bishops Printers Limited

Hugman, B (1998) *The PFA Premier & Football League Players Records 1946–2006*, Hertfordshire: Queen Anne Press

Hutchenson, J (1982) *The Football Industry*, Glasgow: R. Drew

Inglis, S (1987) *The Football Grounds of Great Britain*, London: Willow

Inglis, S (1988) *League Football and the Men who Made It*, London: HarperCollinsWillow

Jeffs, P, Farmery, C, and Owen, R (1998) *Portsmouth Football Club 1898–1998: The Official Centenary Pictorial History*, Portsmouth: Bishops Printers Limited,

Johnston, F (ed.) (1934) *The Football Encyclopaedia*, London: Associated Sporting Press

Joyce, N (2004) *Football League Players' Records 1888–1939*, Nottingham: Soccer Data

Juson, D, Aldworth, C, Bendell, B, Bull, D, and Chalk G (2004) *Saints v Pompey: A history of unrelenting rivalry*, Bristol: Hagiology Publishing

Lovesey, P (1970) *The Official Centenary History of the Amateur Athletic Association*, London: Guinness Superlatives

Mallory, J (1997) *Football League Tables*, Glasgow and London: Collins

Mason, T (1980) *Association Football and English Society 1863–1915*, Brighton: Harvester Press

Neasom, M, Cooper, M and Robinson, D (1997) *Pompey: The History of Portsmouth Football Club*, Portsmouth: Milestone Publications

Oliver, G (1995) *World Soccer* (2nd ed), Bath: Guinness

Revins, R (1933) *The Old Hammers – Personalities and Reminiscences of Boleyn Castle Silver Jubilee*: Stratford, London: Balthrope

Robertson, J (1905) *Advice to the Budding Left Half in Football and How to Play It. By Champions of the Game*, London and Dundee

Shaoul, M, and Williamson, T (2000) *Forever England – A History of the National Side*, Gloucestershire: Tempus

Wall, F (1935) *Fifty Years of Football*, London: Cassel & Co.